Seaboard To Sideboard

Entertains

Seaboard To Sideboard
Entertains

A collection of

recipes from the

Junior League

of Wilmington,

North Carolina

SEABOARD TO SIDEBOARD ENTERTAINS

Published by the Junior League of Wilmington, North Carolina, Inc.
Copyright © 2011
Junior League of Wilmington, NC
3803 Wrightsville Avenue, #9
Wilmington, North Carolina 28403
910-799-7405

Photography page 12 courtesy of Arlie Gardens
All other photography © by Joshua Curry
Food Styling by Estelle Baker and Executive Chef James Bain
Artwork
Pages 13, 81 © by Four Seasons Publishing; Page 29 © by Picture Perfect;
Page 43 © by San Lori Design; Pages 57, 69, 121, 137 © by Odd Balls;
Page 93 © by Spare Bedroom Design; Page 105 © by Anna Griffin, Inc.;
Page 121 © by Putnam House; Page 147 © by Crane & Co.

Library of Congress Control Number: 2009931022
ISBN: 978-0-9607822-1-5

Edited, Designed, and Produced by

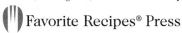 Favorite Recipes® Press
An imprint of

FRP.INC

A wholly owned subsidiary of Southwestern/Great American, Inc.
P.O. Box 305142
Nashville, Tennessee 37230
800-358-0560

Art Director and Book Design: Steve Newman
Project Editor: Tanis Westbrook

Manufactured in the United States of America
First Printing: 2011
10,000 copies

THE JUNIOR LEAGUE OF WILMINGTON, NC, INC.

OUR MISSION

Empowering women to enrich and improve our community
through their leadership as trained volunteers.

OUR VISION

To be a fiscally sound, leading nonprofit with a growing membership that creates
positive and measurable change in our community.

OUR CORE VALUES

A commitment to service
Prudent fiscal responsibility and management
Accountability to community and each other
Individual and organizational integrity through open and honest communication
Attitude of gratitude and mutual respect for each other

ABOUT US

The Junior League of Wilmington, NC, Inc., is a member of the Association of Junior Leagues
International (AJLI), a global organization composed of more than 290 Leagues in the U.S., Canada,
United Kingdom, and Mexico with over 193,000 members. Since 1901 Junior Leagues have provided
communities with volunteers who are concerned, committed, and resourceful. We continually develop,
fund and implement programs to improve our communities. The Junior League offers women a unique
and powerful way to make a difference and become community leaders.

The Junior League of Wilmington, North Carolina, Inc., was formed in 1952 as an outgrowth of
the Charity League, which began in 1923 to support the social welfare workers in the county. Cookbooks
have long been a tradition in the League as a strategy to raise funds to support projects and programs that
are impactful in the local community. As trained leaders and volunteers, members currently support the
education of children and teens through 15,000 hours of fund-raising and community service activities
each year. Cookbook sales are a primary fund-raising activity for the League, and this purchase of *Seaboard
to Sideboard Entertains* contributes to the impact that we hope to achieve. The League is grateful for your
support of our efforts.

FOREWORD

Celia Rivenbark

As casual as a pig-pickin' in the backyard with paper plates and folding tables borrowed from the church, or as elegant as a formal dinner on finest china in the high-ceilinged dining room of an antebellum mansion, entertaining in Wilmington is delightfully diverse.

Lucky enough to live on the Cape Fear Coast, most Wilmingtonians can, with a moment's notice, throw together a shrimp boil, a fish fry, or an oyster roast with suitable side dishes. Culinary celebrations along Cape Fear are delicious, memorable, and filled with laughter and tall tales. It's hard not to be hospitable when you have Stump Sound oysters on hand, after all.

Cape Fear cooks make it look easy, almost effortless, which is the real trick to keeping company at ease while enjoying your own party. There is plain, and there is fancy, but the bottom line is that it is all delectable.

In the South, we know that food equals love. That is why we think nothing of baking a from-scratch mile-high pound cake to take to a friend who needs cheering up. Many of us Southerners can rattle off at least a dozen different deviled egg recipes because we've lovingly served them at weddings and wakes alike.

In *Seaboard to Sideboard Entertains*, you'll sample the finest flavors of the area's best cooks. From the delicate bridal shower-worthy Cucumber-Watercress Tea Sandwiches to hearty appetizers like Hot Swiss Bacon Dip and zesty Blue Cheese Bread, it's all here. Grilled Fruit Kabobs, succulent Buttermilk Fried Chicken, densely divine Rum Cake . . . the only agony is deciding which to try first.

While there are plenty of traditional Southern favorites—savory Cape Fear Crab Cakes, comforting Peanut and Edamame Stew, and scrumptious Shrimp and Grits for instance—there's also a nod to the modern gastronome. Pear and Smoked Gouda Salad, anyone? Yes, please!

Sure, it's a beautiful cookbook, but as any good Southern cook knows, new and shiny isn't always best. Like its predecessor, *Seaboard to Sideboard*, this is a cookbook that will become dog-eared and even a bit splattered as you return to it time and again. The pages will be wonderfully worn, notes scribbled in margins reminding you that a recipe is "Mom's favorite," or "Perfect for picnics," or simply "Best Ever!"

This will be that cookbook, the one that you pull off the shelf when company's coming (even if that company is just a very special party of one!).

Happy hosting, y'all.

Celia Rivenbark is an award-winning author, newspaper columnist, and humorist who lives, and cooks, in the Cape Fear region. She added a few of her own delectable Southern dishes to this recipe collection. The Junior League of Wilmington appreciates her warm support.

ACKNOWLEDGMENTS

The Junior League of Wilmington, NC, Inc., would like to thank the following special artisans whose collective talents helped to produce more than just a book. Because of their generosity of time and spirit, this project became a work of beauty that can just as easily sit on the coffee table as the kitchen counter. We are grateful that these extraordinary individuals allowed us to showcase their gifts for our readers to enjoy.

JOSHUA CURRY is a passionate, experienced photographer with a sophisticated portfolio of images that illustrate his artistic eye for composition, color, lighting, and mood. Inspired by the experience of growing up on the North Carolina coast and his Wrightsville Beach hometown, Josh knew at an early age that he would follow an artistic path, immersing himself in the context of his subjects, from a U.S. president on the campaign trail to local surfers. Josh has captured the spirit of many local celebrities, minted the look of up-and-coming fashion models, established iconic compact disc covers for emerging musicians, and illustrated the works of craftsmen and chefs. In *Seaboard to Sideboard Entertains*, he masters the essence of still life via the featured delectable edibles and at the same time captures the brilliance of the inviting event scenery.

ESTELLE BAKER is the owner of The Fisherman's Wife, a gift shop full of little luxuries. The shop provides a delightful, delicate balance of home furnishings, individually styled paper and invitations, and treasures to be kept or shared. Since 1992 locals have counted on Estelle and her staff to procure the most distinctive gifts and decorative accessories. The heritage of the coastal region is apparent from the moment a shopper steps foot on the quaint front porch. The Fisherman's Wife was involved in the original *Seaboard to Sideboard* cookbook, and Estelle and her team demonstrated their continuing support for the Junior League of Wilmington by donating and styling the table pieces and the invitations for *Seaboard to Sideboard Entertains*. Their eye for the artistic side of entertaining is unparalleled. Estelle and her staff help hosts succeed with their entertaining efforts through gorgeous decorative accessories that take their cues from the picturesque coast.

JAMES BAIN is Executive Chef of the Dockside Restaurant and Marina at Wrightsville Beach, North Carolina. He grew up in the Cape Fear region and involved himself in cooking, surfing, and pioneering his own style of coastal cuisine. James graduated with honors from the premiere culinary school Johnson and Wales University, and for over twenty years he has subsequently delighted locals with his creation of restaurants and menus that showcase the local seafood treats. He shares his expertise through cooking classes, segments on local morning shows, and culinary events. James' commitment to the waterman's way of life is reflected in his desire to catch and cook indigenous seafood. He emphasizes responsibility for sustainable seafood, environmental conscientiousness, and education to the public about the palatable recipe ingredients to be found in the local region. In *Seaboard to Sideboard Entertains*, James graciously shares his talents in the gastronomic arts through the offerings of some of his favorite recipes, for all to savor.

Contents

Oyster Roast
January
10

Progressive Dinners
February
22

Southern Showers
March
34

Garden Party
April
44

Porch Parties
May
56

Boxed Lunch at the Beach
June
68

4th of July by the Water

July

78

Summer Suppers

August

88

Carolina Traditions

September

100

Pig Pickin'

October

112

Flotilla Party

November

124

Holiday Traditions

December

136

Sponsors 152

Contributors 153

Index 155

Oyster Roast

The Annual Low Country Oyster Roast at Airlie Gardens is a prototype of the classic feast of local seafood and fixin's. Along the Cape Fear Coast, the oyster is valued for its savory taste instead of its potential to produce a pearl! Raw or steamed oysters, slurped straight from the shell, are a local delicacy, though you need rubber gloves and a good knife to pop those shells open deftly. Months with an "r," according to folklore, are the best harvesting times, and feasts of oysters on New Year's Day are supposed to bring good luck for the year. So January is a great time to celebrate this treasured bivalve mollusk.

Airlie's Oyster Roast each year is one of many enjoyable events at this local historic garden. Airlie Gardens was part of a 640-acre land grant from King George II to the Ogden brothers in 1735. By the 1790s, much of the original acreage had been transferred to Joshua Grainger Wright, first president of the Bank of Cape Fear and Speaker of the North Carolina House of Representatives. In 1835 Mount Lebanon Chapel, still in use today, was built on the property; it is listed on the National Register of Historical Places. In 1884 Pembroke and Sarah Jones, wealthy industrialists from New York and relatives of the Wrights, purchased a parcel of land that Mrs. Jones would eventually transform into a garden estate, with lakes and tree-lined paths. The Jones' considerable influence in society at the turn of the century appears to be the genesis of the popular saying "keeping up with the Joneses," because of their lavish style of entertaining.

The Corbett family, local business owners with strong ties to the community, purchased the Airlie property in 1948 and maintained the gardens as they had been developed originally. A visit to the Gardens in the spring season became a tradition, or as some would say, a pilgrimage, to view the 100,000 blooming azaleas and 50,000 camellias in full glory. Working with a grant from the Clean Water Management Trust Fund, New Hanover County bought sixty-seven acres of the Airlie property in 1998, so that the Gardens could be preserved as an historic public garden. Now successful events are enjoyed by residents and visitors throughout the year, with a special highlight being the Annual Oyster Roast.

Jones' Annual Oyster Roast

Please join us to
Welcome
the
New Year

January 1st
5 o'clock

Summer Rest Road

Sadie & Pembroke

no regrets!

Oyster Roast

Mulled Red Wine   14

Cheddar en Croûte   14

Crab and Artichoke Dip   15

Hot Swiss Bacon Dip   15

Oyster Sauce   16

Low Country EZ Oyster Stew   16

Cream of Oyster Stew   17

Wrightsville Beach Oyster Stew   17

Seafood Pot   18

Brunswick Stew   19

Quick-and-Easy Fried Oysters   20

Oyster Stuffing   20

Cheesecake Brownies   21

Oatmeal Caramel Cranberry Cookies   21

MULLED RED WINE

1	(750-milliliter) bottle red wine
1/4	cup raw sugar
1	stick cinnamon
5	whole cloves
1	tablespoon nutmeg

Juice of 1 orange

Orange zest curls for garnish

6	to 8 sticks cinnamon for garnish

Pour the wine into a medium saucepan. Stir in the raw sugar. Add one cinnamon stick, the cloves and nutmeg or tie in a piece of cheesecloth before adding. Stir in the orange juice. Heat until warm and frothy. Do not boil. Strain into serving cups. Garnish each serving with orange curls and one cinnamon stick.

Serves 6 to 8

CHEDDAR EN CROÛTE

2	(8-count) packages refrigerator crescent rolls
8	ounces sharp Cheddar cheese, shredded
1/2	cup packed brown sugar
1/4	cup (1/2 stick) butter, melted

Unroll one package of the dough into a rectangle on a baking sheet, pressing the perforations to seal. Sprinkle with the cheese, leaving a 1-inch border. Sprinkle with the brown sugar. Unroll the remaining dough, pressing the perforations to seal. Place over the top of the cheese layer, crimping the edges of the dough to seal. Brush with the butter. Bake in a preheated 350-degree oven for 20 to 25 minutes or until golden brown and the cheese melts. Serve warm.

Serves 12 to 15

CRAB AND ARTICHOKE DIP

1/2 cup minced onion

1 tablespoon butter

16 ounces cream cheese

1 teaspoon Worcestershire sauce

1 teaspoon horseradish sauce

1/2 teaspoon Old Bay seasoning

5 dashes of Tabasco sauce

1 (14-ounce) can artichoke hearts

8 ounces crab meat, shells removed and meat flaked

1/4 cup (1 ounce) grated Parmesan cheese

Sauté the onion in the butter in a saucepan until soft but not brown. Add the cream cheese. Cook over low heat until soft, stirring constantly. Add the Worcestershire sauce, horseradish sauce, Old Bay seasoning and Tabasco sauce and stir until blended. Fold in the artichoke hearts and crab meat. Pour into a shallow baking dish (1 1/2 inches deep). Sprinkle the Parmesan cheese evenly over the top. Bake in a preheated 400-degree oven for 30 minutes or until bubbly on the sides and brown on top. Serve with crackers or crostini.

Serves 6 to 8

HOT SWISS BACON DIP

1/2 cup low-fat mayonnaise

8 ounces low-fat cream cheese, softened

1 cup (4 ounces) shredded Swiss cheese

3 tablespoons finely chopped green onions

1 pound bacon, cooked and crumbled

1/2 sleeve butter crackers, crushed

3 tablespoons butter, melted

Mix the mayonnaise, cream cheese and Swiss cheese in a bowl. Stir in the green onions and bacon. Spread in a shallow 8×8-inch baking dish. Sprinkle with the crackers. Drizzle with the butter. Bake in a preheated 350-degree oven for 20 to 25 minutes or until heated through. Serve hot with crackers.

Serves 10 to 12

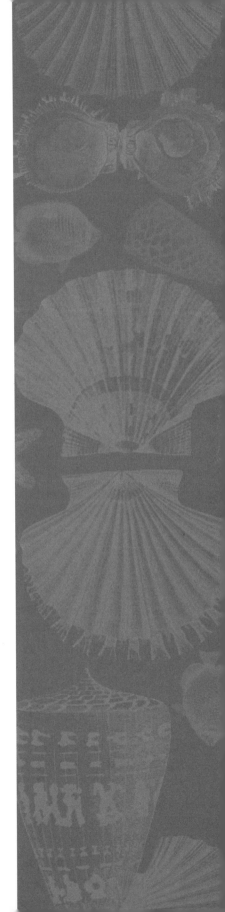

Oyster Sauce

1   tablespoon chili sauce
1   tablespoon fresh lemon juice
5   drops of Tabasco sauce
1/2   teaspoon celery salt
5   drops of Worcestershire sauce

Mix the chili sauce, lemon juice, Tabasco sauce, celery salt and Worcestershire sauce in the order listed in a bowl. Serve over raw or cooked oysters.

Serves 6

Low Country EZ Oyster Stew

1   pint shucked oysters with oyster liquor
1/4   cup (1/2 stick) butter
1   quart (4 cups) whole milk
Pinch of salt
Pinch of pepper
Seafood seasoning to taste

Cook the undrained oysters in a 4-quart saucepan over low heat until the edges of the oysters just begin to curl. Add the butter, milk, salt and pepper. Heat until hot; do not boil or the oysters will become tough. Ladle into soup bowls and sprinkle with seafood seasoning.

Makes about 6 cups

CREAM OF OYSTER STEW

1	pint shucked oysters with oyster liquor	1/4	teaspoon white pepper
1/4	cup (1/2 stick) butter	1	(10-ounce) can cream of mushroom soup
1/2	cup chopped celery	1/2	cup milk
1/2	cup chopped onion	1/4	cup chopped parsley
1/2	cup chopped asparagus		

Drain the oysters, reserving the liquor. Melt the butter in a 2-quart saucepan. Add the celery, onion and asparagus and sauté for 5 minutes. Add the white pepper and the reserved oyster liquor. Add the soup and milk and stir until smooth. Bring to a low simmer. Add the parsley and oysters. Cook until the oysters are plump and the edges begin to curl. Ladle into soup bowls. Add a splash of sherry just before serving for more flavor.

Makes 5 cups

WRIGHTSVILLE BEACH OYSTER STEW

1	cup (2 sticks) butter	1 1/2	teaspoons thyme
4	small onions, chopped	1 1/2	teaspoons pepper
1	bunch celery, chopped	1 1/4	teaspoons salt
8	ounces sliced mushrooms	1/2	gallon (8 cups) milk
1/4	teaspoon minced fresh garlic	1/2	gallon (8 cups) heavy cream
1 1/2	cups all-purpose flour	1	gallon shucked oysters with oyster liquor
1	(2-ounce) jar pimento		

Melt the butter in a large stockpot over medium heat. Add the onions, celery, mushrooms and garlic and sauté until tender. Reduce the heat to low. Add the flour, undrained pimento, thyme, pepper and salt. Cook for 3 minutes, stirring constantly. Add the milk, cream and undrained oysters. Simmer for 30 minutes or until the edges of the oysters curl. Do not boil. Ladle into soup bowls.

Serves 10 to 12

SEAFOOD POT

1/3	cup extra-virgin olive oil
1	onion, sliced
1	tablespoon minced garlic
2 1/2	cups dry white wine
1	(29-ounce) can diced fire-roasted tomatoes
1	(28-ounce) can crushed tomatoes
1	cup clam juice
2	cups chicken stock or seafood stock
3/4	teaspoon crushed red pepper flakes
3	tablespoons chopped flat-leaf parsley
16	cherrystone clams
16	mussels
12	sea scallops
12	ounces wahoo or other mild white fish, cut into 1-inch chunks
1	pound calamari rings
16	medium shrimp

Heat the olive oil in a large stockpot. Add the onion and garlic and sauté for 5 minutes. Add the wine, fire-roasted tomatoes, crushed tomatoes, clam juice, stock, red pepper flakes and parsley. Simmer for 40 minutes. Stir in the clams and mussels gently. Add the scallops, fish, calamari and shrimp. Simmer for 10 minutes. Discard any mussels or clams that do not open. Ladle into soup bowls. Serve with warm crusty bread.

Serves 8

BRUNSWICK STEW

1	large rotisserie chicken or cooked whole chicken
3	onions, chopped
1/4	cup (1/2 stick) butter
2	pounds pulled pork
4	(16-ounce) cans tomatoes
6	tablespoons Worcestershire sauce
3 1/2	cups ketchup
3	tablespoons hot pepper sauce
2	bay leaves
1/2	(12-ounce) bottle chili sauce
1	teaspoon dry mustard
3	tablespoons vinegar
1	(16-ounce) package frozen tiny lima beans
1	(16-ounce) package frozen corn
1	(8-ounce) package frozen green peas
1	(8-ounce) package frozen okra
4	potatoes, chopped

Shred the chicken, discarding the skin and bones. Sauté the onions in the butter in a heavy stockpot until translucent. Add the chicken, pork, tomatoes, Worcestershire sauce, ketchup, hot sauce, bay leaves, chili sauce, dry mustard, vinegar, lima beans, corn, green peas, okra and potatoes and mix well. Cook for 1 hour, stirring occasionally. Discard the bay leaves. Ladle into soup bowls.

Serves 16

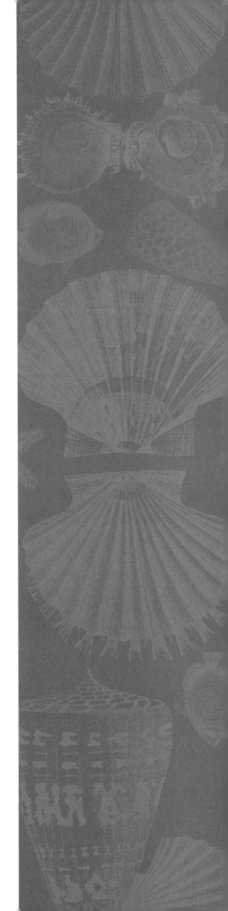

QUICK-AND-EASY FRIED OYSTERS

1   to 2 cups baking mix
1   pint shucked oysters, drained
Peanut oil for deep-frying
Salt to taste

Place the baking mix in a large shallow bowl. Add the oysters a few at a time and toss lightly to coat well. Place in a wire basket and shake to remove the excess coating. Fry in preheated 350-degree peanut oil in a deep fryer for 1 1/2 to 2 minutes or until golden brown. Drain on paper towels. Repeat with the remaining oysters. Sprinkle with salt. Serve with cocktail sauce or tartar sauce. The oysters may also be fried in 1 to 2 inches of preheated 350-degree peanut oil in a large skillet.

Serves 4

OYSTER STUFFING

1   pound bulk pork sausage
1   (16-ounce) package unseasoned dry bread stuffing mix
1   dozen shucked oysters, with oyster liquor
2   cups chopped celery
1   onion, chopped
1/4   cup (1/2 stick) butter, melted
1 1/2 cups turkey broth
Salt and pepper to taste
Seafood seasoning to taste

Brown the sausage in a large deep skillet over medium-high heat, stirring until crumbly. Combine the undrained sausage with the stuffing mix in a large bowl and mix well. Stir in the undrained oysters, celery, onion and butter. Stir in enough of the broth to moisten the mixture without being soggy. Season with salt, pepper and seafood seasoning. Chill in the refrigerator. Use to stuff a turkey just before roasting. For a healthier alternative, use turkey sausage instead of pork sausage.

Makes enough stuffing for 1 turkey

CHEESECAKE BROWNIES

2	cups sugar	1	teaspoon baking powder
4	eggs	1/2	teaspoon salt
1 1/3	cups vegetable oil	8	ounces cream cheese,
4	ounces unsweetened		softened
	chocolate, melted	1/3	cup sugar
2	teaspoons vanilla extract	1	egg
2	cups all-purpose flour	1/2	teaspoon vanilla extract

Beat 2 cups sugar and 4 eggs in a mixing bowl until light. Add the oil, chocolate and 2 teaspoons vanilla and mix well. Add the flour, baking powder and salt and mix until smooth. The batter will be thick. Reserve 3/4 cup of the batter. Pour the remaining batter into a greased 9×13-inch baking pan. Beat the cream cheese, 1/3 cup sugar, 1 egg and 1/2 teaspoon vanilla in a mixing bowl until smooth. Pour over the batter. Drop the reserved 3/4 cup batter over the top and swirl with a knife to marbleize. Bake in a preheated 350-degree oven for 45 to 55 minutes or until the brownies pull away from the sides of the pan.

Serves 12 to 24

OATMEAL CARAMEL CRANBERRY COOKIES

1 3/4	cups all-purpose flour	3/4	cup packed brown sugar
1	teaspoon baking soda	2	eggs
1	teaspoon salt	1/2	cup dried cranberries
3	cups rolled oats	1	cup (6 ounces) dark
1	cup (2 sticks) unsalted		chocolate chips (optional)
	butter, softened	1	(6-ounce) package
3/4	cup granulated sugar or		toffee bits
	equivalent amount of	1 1/4	teaspoons Madagascar
	sugar substitute		vanilla extract

Mix the flour, baking soda, salt and oats together. Beat the butter in a large mixing bowl until creamy. Add the granulated sugar and brown sugar gradually, beating constantly until light and fluffy. Add the eggs one at a time, beating until well combined after each addition. Beat in the flour mixture gradually. Fold in the cranberries, chocolate chips, toffee bits and vanilla. Drop by spoonfuls onto a cookie sheet. Bake in a preheated 350-degree oven for 10 to 12 minutes or until brown. Cool on the cookie sheet for 5 minutes. Remove to wire racks to cool completely.

Makes 1 dozen

Progressive Dinners

Sharing food and drink with friends can provide warmth and comfort in the colder winter months. By February, coastal residents are getting excited about the impending spring weather, but we still have to endure some cold spells. What fun to come out of winter hibernation to warm up with comfort food and good friends! A progressive dinner makes hosting easy, because no one has to do all the cooking (or cleaning)! Appetizers at one friend's home, soup or salad at another, and two more comrades offering a main dish and then dessert. Maybe someone could even serve the children's meal. Dinner party etiquette, such as that requisite bottle of wine for your host, no longer applies for the progressive dinner, since everyone is contributing.

February provides a number of incentives and potential themes for getting together to share enjoyable moments with close acquaintances, including Valentine's Day, President's Day weekend, Groundhog Day, and even perhaps a Super Bowl Sunday! Locally, the Children's Museum of Wilmington's Circle of Friends has historically held its "Feeding Friend-zy" fund-raising event in February, which is a twist on traditional progressive dinners. Several theme-based parties at homes combine into one event later in the evening at the museum for dessert and camaraderie. However you choose to entertain and spend time with friends, comfort food is always on the menu in a progressive dinner. Moving from one person's home to the next allows for more digestion time too, so you can enjoy even more gustatory delights!

Join Susan and Lee

for a

"Feeding Friend-zy" Chili Supper

Saturday, February 18th

7:00 p.m.

11312 Market Street

please respond

dessert following

Wilmington Children's Museum

Progressive Dinners

Bacon Almond Crostini   26

Creamy Olive Spread   26

Hummus   27

Eggplant Caviar   27

Blue Cheese Bread   28

Spinach Salad   28

Peanut and Edamame Stew   29

White Chicken Chili   30

Creamy Chicken and Broccoli Bake   30

Spinach Lasagna with White Sauce   31

Mini Meat Loaves   31

Oven-Roasted Asparagus   32

Red-Skinned Potatoes with Herbs   32

Peanut Butter Pie   33

Chocolate Pecan Squares   33

BACON ALMOND CROSTINI

1	baguette
1	teaspoon butter, melted
1/4	cup slivered almonds, toasted
2	tablespoons chopped green onions
2	slices bacon, cooked and crumbled
1/2	cup (or less) mayonnaise
1	cup (4 ounces) shredded Monterey Jack cheese

Cut the baguette into 1/2-inch slices. Brush with the butter and place on a baking sheet. Bake in a preheated 400-degree oven for 5 minutes. Maintain the oven temperature. Mix the almonds, green onions, bacon, mayonnaise and cheese in a bowl. Spread over the toasted baguette slices. Bake for 5 minutes and serve immediately.

Makes 3 dozen

CREAMY OLIVE SPREAD

16	ounces cream cheese, softened
1	(5-ounce) can chopped black olives, drained
1/2	cup chopped green olives with pimentos
2	tablespoons garlic-infused olive oil
2	tablespoons fresh lemon juice

Salt to taste

Combine the cream cheese, black olives, green olives, olive oil, lemon juice and salt in a bowl and mix well. Chill, covered, for 1 to 2 hours or until the flavors meld. Remove from the refrigerator and let stand for 30 minutes or until softened. Serve with pita chips or other crunchy mild crackers.

Serves 8

HUMMUS

2   (15-ounce) cans garbanzo beans, drained and rinsed
4   garlic cloves
1/3 cup olive oil
1/2 cup lemon juice
1/3 cup water
2   to 3 tablespoons tahini
3/4 teaspoon salt
1/2 teaspoon pepper
1/4 teaspoon allspice
1/4 cup chopped parsley for garnish
1/4 teaspoon paprika for garnish

Process the beans, garlic, olive oil, lemon juice, water, tahini, salt, pepper and allspice in a food processor until blended. Spoon into a deep platter. Garnish with parsley and paprika. Serve with pita chips or crackers.

Serves 4 to 6

EGGPLANT CAVIAR

1   eggplant
3   tablespoons olive oil
1   large Vidalia onion, coarsely chopped
3   large tomatoes, coarsely chopped

Prick the entire surface of the egglant with a fork. Place in a baking pan. Bake in a preheated 350-degree oven for 45 minutes or until the skin is wrinkled and brownish purple in color. Remove from the oven to cool. Peel the eggplant and coarsely chop. Heat the olive oil in a large skillet. Add the onion, tomatoes and eggplant. Cook over medium heat for 15 to 20 minutes or until the onion is tender, stirring frequently. Reduce the heat to low. Cook for 30 minutes or until the tomatoes and eggplant are soft. Remove from the heat to cool.
Serve with crackers or French bread.

Serves 12

BLUE CHEESE BREAD

1	(8-count) can refrigerator biscuits
1/3	cup butter
3	tablespoons crumbled blue cheese

Sesame seeds to taste

Cut the biscuit dough into quarters. Layer the biscuit dough quarters in a greased baking pan. Melt the butter and blue cheese in a saucepan over low heat, stirring frequently. Drizzle over the biscuit dough. Sprinkle with sesame seeds. Bake in a preheated 375-degree oven until golden brown.

Serves 4

SPINACH SALAD

1/2	cup vegetable oil
1/3	cup ketchup
1/4	cup apple cider vinegar
1	tablespoon Worcestershire sauce
1/2	teaspoon salt
1	red onion, chopped
18	ounces baby spinach leaves, rinsed and dried
4	hard-cooked eggs, sliced
6	slices bacon, cooked and crumbled
8	mushrooms, sliced

Mix the oil, ketchup, vinegar, Worcestershire sauce, salt and onion in a sealable container. Chill, covered, for 3 to 10 hours. Combine the spinach, hard-cooked eggs, bacon and mushrooms in a salad bowl. Add one-half of the dressing and toss to coat. Serve with the remaining dressing on the side.

Serves 6 to 8

PEANUT AND EDAMAME STEW

1   tablespoon olive oil
1 1/2   cups coarsely chopped yellow onion
        (about 1 large)
1   green bell pepper, coarsely chopped
1/2   cup shredded carrots
1/2   cup chopped celery (about 1 stalk)
3   garlic cloves
2   tablespoons minced peeled ginger
1   tablespoon curry powder
1   (14-ounce) can tomatoes, drained
1   bay leaf
5   cups vegetable broth or chicken broth
1   pound sweet potatoes, peeled and chopped
1 1/2   cups shelled edamame
1/4   cup creamy or chunky natural peanut butter
1/4   cup cilantro, chopped
6   ounces baby spinach, coarsely chopped
Coarse salt and pepper to taste

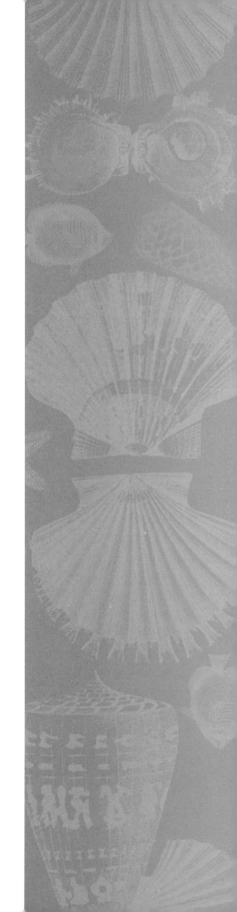

Heat the olive oil in a 4-quart saucepan or Dutch oven over medium heat. Add the onion, bell pepper, carrots and celery. Sauté for 5 minutes or until soft and translucent. Add the garlic, ginger and curry powder. Sauté for 1 minute or until fragrant. Do not brown the garlic. Add the tomatoes and bay leaf. Cook, uncovered, for 3 minutes or until the tomatoes are slightly reduced. Add the broth and sweet potatoes. Bring to a boil. Reduce the heat to low and simmer for 8 minutes. Stir in the edamame and peanut butter until combined. Cook for 2 minutes or until heated through. Stir in the cilantro and spinach. Cook until the spinach wilts. Season with coarse salt and pepper. Discard the bay leaf. Ladle into soup bowls.

Serves 8

White Chicken Chili

1	small onion, chopped	2	(4-ounce) cans chopped
1/2	teaspoon garlic powder		green chiles
Vegetable oil		1	teaspoon salt
1	pound cooked chicken,	1	teaspoon ground cumin
	cut into chunks	1	teaspoon oregano
2	(15-ounce) cans Great	1/2	teaspoon black pepper
	Northern beans,	1/4	teaspoon cayenne pepper
	drained and rinsed	1	cup fat-free sour cream
1	(14-ounce) can fat-free	1/2	cup whipping cream
	chicken broth		

Sauté the onion and garlic powder in a small amount of oil in a stockpot until the onion is translucent. Add the chicken, beans, broth, green chiles, salt, cumin, oregano, black pepper and cayenne pepper and mix well. Bring to a boil. Reduce the heat to low and simmer, uncovered, for 35 minutes. Stir in the sour cream and whipping cream just before serving. Ladle into soup bowls and sprinkle with shredded Cheddar cheese.

Serves 4 to 6

Creamy Chicken and Broccoli Bake

1	(16-ounce) package frozen broccoli florets	1/2	cup mayonnaise
		1/2	cup milk
3	boneless skinless chicken breasts, cooked and chopped	3	tablespoons lemon juice
		3	cups (12 ounces) shredded sharp Cheddar cheese
1	(10-ounce) can cream of chicken soup	2	cups cornbread stuffing mix
1	(10-ounce) can cream of mushroom soup	1/4	cup (1/2 stick) butter, melted

Place the broccoli in a microwave-safe dish. Microwave, covered, for 5 minutes; drain. Arrange in a baking dish. Top with the chicken. Combine the soups, mayonnaise, milk and lemon juice in a bowl and mix well. Pour over the chicken. Sprinkle with the cheese. Combine the stuffing mix and butter in a bowl and mix well. Sprinkle over the cheese. Bake in a preheated 350-degree oven for 40 minutes or until bubbly.

Serves 8

SPINACH LASAGNA WITH WHITE SAUCE

1	(10-ounce) package frozen chopped spinach	1/2	cup skim milk
2	cups part-skim ricotta cheese	6	lasagna noodles
1	egg, beaten	8	ounces mushrooms, sliced
1	(29-ounce) jar Alfredo pasta sauce	1/2	cup (2 ounces) shredded mozzarella cheese

Place the spinach in a microwave-safe bowl. Microwave on High for 4 minutes. Stir in the ricotta cheese. Add the egg and mix well. Blend the pasta sauce and milk together in a bowl. Spread 1/2 cup of the sauce mixture evenly in a 10×15-inch baking pan coated with nonstick cooking spray. Layer the noodles, spinach mixture and mushrooms one-half at a time in the prepared pan. Pour the remaining sauce over the top. Sprinkle with the mozzarella cheese.

Spray a sheet of foil with nonstick cooking spray. Place sprayed side down over the lasagna and seal tightly. Bake in a preheated 350-degree oven for 50 to 60 minutes or until cooked through. Remove from the oven and uncover. Spoon some of the sauce over any exposed noodles. Turn off the oven. Return the uncovered dish to the warm oven and let stand for 15 minutes. Serve at once or let stand until ready to serve.

Serves 8

MINI MEAT LOAVES

1/2	cup ketchup	1/4	cup seasoned bread crumbs
1 1/2	tablespoons Dijon mustard	1/2	teaspoon salt
1	pound ground beef	1/2	teaspoon oregano
3/4	cup chopped onion	1/8	teaspoon pepper
		1	egg, lightly beaten

Whisk the ketchup and Dijon mustard together in a bowl. Reserve 1/4 cup of the ketchup mixture. Add the ground beef, onion, bread crumbs, salt, oregano, pepper and egg to the remaining ketchup mixture and mix well. Divide into four equal portions and shape into loaves. Place on a baking sheet sprayed with nonstick cooking spray. Brush each with the reserved ketchup mixture. Bake in a preheated 400-degree oven for 25 minutes. The meat loaves can also be baked in four miniature loaf pans or one 5×9-inch loaf pan.

Serves 4

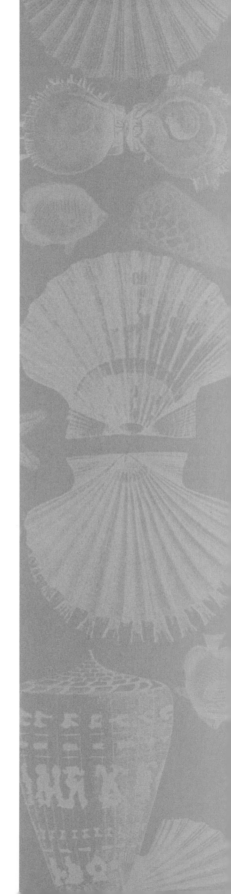

OVEN-ROASTED ASPARAGUS

  1 1/2 pounds fresh asparagus spears, rinsed and trimmed
  2 tablespoons chopped fresh herbs, or
        2 teaspoons crushed dried Italian seasoning
  2 tablespoons canola oil
  Pinch of salt
  Pinch of pepper

Toss the asparagus with the herbs, canola oil, salt and pepper in a large bowl. Arrange in a single layer on a baking parchment-lined 10×15-inch baking sheet. Roast in a preheated 450-degree oven for 10 to 12 minutes, stirring once. Remove from the oven. Remove the asparagus with tongs to a serving platter.

Serves 4 to 6

RED-SKINNED POTATOES WITH HERBS

  6 cups unpeeled red potatoes, cut into 1-inch pieces
  1 tablespoon fresh thyme
  3 tablespoons chopped fresh sweet basil
  Salt to taste
  4 ounces cream cheese
  1 1/4 cups (5 ounces) shredded sharp Cheddar cheese
  1/2 cup half-and-half
  1/2 teaspoon salt
  1/4 teaspoon pepper

Place the potatoes in a 3-quart saucepan. Add enough water to almost cover. Add the thyme, basil and salt to taste. Simmer, covered, until tender, stirring occasionally. Drain, being careful to retain the herbs. Heat over low heat for 1 to 2 minutes to dry the potatoes, shaking the saucepan constantly. Add the cream cheese, Cheddar cheese, half-and-half, 1/2 teaspoon salt and the pepper. Heat until the cheeses melt, stirring constantly.

Serves 4 to 6

PEANUT BUTTER PIE

8 ounces cream cheese, softened
1 cup chunky peanut butter
1 1/2 cups sifted confectioners' sugar
16 ounces whipped topping
2 (9-inch) graham cracker pie shells
Shaved chocolate for garnish

Beat the cream cheese and peanut butter in a large mixing bowl until light and fluffy. Add the confectioners' sugar gradually, beating constantly. Fold in the whipped topping. Spoon into the pie shells. Freeze, covered, for 8 hours or longer. Garnish with shaved chocolate.

Makes 2 pies

CHOCOLATE PECAN SQUARES

1 cup packed light brown sugar
2 1/2 cups all-purpose flour
1/2 cup vegetable oil
3 eggs
1 teaspoon baking powder
1 teaspoon salt
1 teaspoon vanilla extract
1 cup (6 ounces) semisweet chocolate chips
1 cup chopped pecans

Combine the brown sugar, flour, oil, eggs, baking powder, salt and vanilla in a bowl and mix well. Stir in the chocolate chips and pecans. Spoon into a greased 9×13-inch baking pan. Bake in a preheated 350-degree oven for 25 to 30 minutes or until the edges pull from the side of the pan. Remove from the oven and cut into squares.

Serves 36

Southern Showers

The themed bridal and baby showers of today became popular during the baby boom following World War II, when the number of both weddings and births increased rapidly. However, the tradition of bestowing gifts upon couples at the time of their union, and as their family grows, originated long ago. Historians have discovered evidence in ancient Roman and Egyptian artifacts suggesting that community members would celebrate weddings and births with gifts and feasts. In fact, gifts for a newborn baby were often handmade, which is consistent with modern customs of making baby quilts and blankets.

Modern bridal showers appear to be related to the historical bridal dowry practice. Lore holds that a young Dutch girl from a prominent family in the 1500s or 1600s wanted to marry a man whose family was working-class. The girl's father feared that the young man would not be able to provide for his daughter, so the father refused to provide the girl's dowry, in hopes that the two would realize that they could not start a home without that support. The townspeople, knowing that the man had a good heart, supported the union by "showering" the girl with gifts to essentially make up a dowry. The father finally approved of the union when he witnessed the town treating the poor man with such high esteem, and he consented to the marriage and completed the girl's dowry. Since then, it has become custom to shower a bride-to-be with gifts to support her journey from single womanhood to starting a family home.

Bridal and baby showers are quintessential events for Southern women. These occasions provide an opportunity to showcase Southern charm through edible delights and an inviting party atmosphere. The birth of a baby is cause for celebration, and spring and summer at the beach inspire possibilities for wedding events, including the parties that allow friends and family to shower their loved ones with gifts and warm wishes. The food is always a central feature of any Southern shower!

To honor Elizabeth our friend so true

A Southern Shower

with friends like you.

Lunch & toasts & a pretty bouquet-Please bring a gift for her wedding day.
"Something old, something new, something borrowed, something blue
or a lucky six pence in her shoe!"

March twentieth
noon
Cape Fear Country Club

Given with love
"Bunco babes"

Please come!

Southern Showers

Perfect Punch   38

Farmers' Market Dip   38

Blue Crab and Brie Fondue   39

Breakfast Squares   39

Chiles Rellenos Quiche   40

Chicken and Arugula Roll-Ups   40

Ambrosia Salad   41

Sour Cream Banana Bread   41

Southern Pound Cake   42

Lemon Squares   42

Roasted Strawberries with Lemon Butter Cookies and
Mint Whipped Cream   43

PERFECT PUNCH

2   (2-liter) bottles ginger ale, chilled

2   (2-liter) bottles lemon-lime soda, chilled

1   (46-ounce) can pineapple juice

2   (1/2-gallon) containers pineapple and/or lime sherbet

Mix one bottle ginger ale, one bottle lemon-lime soda, one-half of the pineapple juice and one-half of the sherbet in a punch bowl. Add the remaining ginger ale, lemon-lime soda, pineapple juice and sherbet to taste or to replenish the punch.

Serves 30

FARMERS' MARKET DIP

8   ounces cream cheese, softened

5   baby carrots

1   red, green or yellow bell pepper

1   teaspoon minced onion

1   teaspoon parsley

1   garlic clove, minced

Dash of salt

Dash of pepper

1   cup sour cream

1   teaspoon capers

Process the cream cheese, carrots, bell pepper, onion, parsley, garlic, salt, pepper, sour cream and capers in a food processor until blended. Spoon into a small serving bowl. Chill, covered, until serving time. Serve with assorted fresh vegetables or crackers.

Serves 6 to 8

BLUE CRAB AND BRIE FONDUE

1	cup heavy cream
6	ounces jumbo lump crab meat, flaked
4	ounces Brie cheese
1	bunch chives, chopped, or to taste

Zest and juice of 1 lemon

Salt and pepper to taste

1/2	cup (2 ounces) grated Parmigiano-Reggiano cheese
1/4	cup panko (Japanese bread crumbs)

Cook the cream in a small saucepan over medium-high heat until reduced by one-half. Stir in the crab meat. Simmer until heated through. Fold in the Brie cheese and chives. Stir in the lemon zest, lemon juice, salt and pepper. Spoon into a greased 8-ounce baking dish. Sprinkle with one-half of the Parmigiano-Reggiano cheese and the bread crumbs. Sprinkle with the remaining Parmigiano-Reggiano cheese. Broil for 25 to 30 seconds or until golden brown. Serve with toast points or spoon over grilled beef tenderloin.

Serves 4 to 6

BREAKFAST SQUARES

1	large pizza crust dough
4	to 6 medium eggs
1/4	cup (1 ounce) grated Parmesan cheese

Salt and pepper to taste

2	cups chopped cooked bacon, ham or sausage, or a combination of each
3/4	cup (3 ounces) shredded sharp Cheddar cheese
3/4	cup (3 ounces) shredded mozzarella cheese

Press the dough into a rimmed pizza pan. Beat the eggs, Parmesan cheese, salt and pepper in a bowl. Pour over the dough. Sprinkle with the bacon, Cheddar cheese and mozzarella cheese. Bake in a preheated 400-degree oven until bubbly.

Serves 6

CHILES RELLENOS QUICHE

3   (7-ounce) cans chopped green chiles, drained

3   cups (12 ounces) shredded sharp Cheddar cheese

1½ cups (6 ounces) shredded Mexican cheese blend

6   eggs, lightly beaten

1½ cups low-fat baking mix

3   cups low-fat milk or skim milk

1½ cups ricotta cheese

Spread the green chiles, Cheddar cheese and Mexican cheese blend in a 9×13-inch glass baking dish sprayed with nonstick cooking spray. Combine the eggs, baking mix and milk in a bowl and mix well. Stir in the ricotta cheese. Pour over the chile layer. Bake in a preheated 375-degree oven for 30 minutes or until set, covering with foil if the top begins to brown.

Serves 12

CHICKEN AND ARUGULA ROLL-UPS

4   boneless skinless chicken breasts

Dash of salt

Dash of pepper

2   teaspoons paprika

1   bunch arugula

4   ounces cream cheese, finely chopped

2   teaspoons olive oil

Place the chicken smooth sides down on clean, flat work surface. Pound each into 1/4-inch thickness. Sprinkle with salt, pepper and the paprika. Cover each with the arugula and cream cheese. Roll up tightly beginning with the narrow end and secure with wooden picks. Heat the olive oil in a large nonstick ovenproof skillet over medium-high heat. Place the chicken roll-ups seam side down in the hot olive oil. Cook for 4 minutes or until golden brown. Turn the chicken and cook for 4 minutes longer. Place in a preheated 400-degree oven. Bake for 10 to 12 minutes or until cooked through. Remove the wooden picks. Cut into slices crosswise to serve, if desired.

Serves 4

AMBROSIA SALAD

1½ cups drained pineapple tidbits
1½ cups drained mandarin orange slices
1   cup miniature marshmallows
1   cup flaked coconut
1½ cups sour cream
1   cup pecans

Combine the pineapple, mandarin oranges, marshmallows, coconut, sour cream and pecans in a large bowl and mix well. Chill, covered, for 8 to 10 hours. Serve chilled.

Serves 10 to 15

SOUR CREAM BANANA BREAD

2   cups all-purpose flour
2   teaspoons baking powder
1   teaspoon baking soda
½   teaspoon salt
1   cup sugar
8   ounces cream cheese, softened
3   tablespoons margarine, softened
1   egg
½   cup sour cream
2   bananas, mashed
1   tablespoon lemon juice

Mix the flour, baking powder, baking soda and salt together. Cream the sugar, cream cheese and margarine in a mixing bowl until light and fluffy. Add the egg and sour cream. Add the flour mixture and bananas alternately, mixing well after each addition. Stir in the lemon juice. Spoon into four greased and floured miniature loaf pans. Bake in a preheated 375-degree oven for 35 to 40 minutes or until the loaves test done.

Makes 4 miniature loaves

SOUTHERN POUND CAKE

1/2 cup milk	1/2 cup (1 stick) margarine,
1/2 teaspoon lemon extract	softened
1/2 teaspoon vanilla extract	1/2 cup shortening
3 cups sifted all-purpose	3 cups sugar
flour	5 eggs
1/2 teaspoon baking powder	

Mix the milk with the flavorings. Mix the flour and baking powder together. Cream the margarine in a mixing bowl. Add the shortening and sugar and beat until light and fluffy. Add the eggs one at a time, beating well after each addition. Add the milk mixture and flour mixture alternately, beating well after each addition. Pour into a greased tube pan or bundt pan. Place in a cold oven. Bake at 350 degrees for 1 1/4 hours. Cool on a wire rack.

Serves 24

LEMON SQUARES

2 1/2 cups sifted all-purpose	4 eggs, beaten
flour	2 cups granulated sugar
1/2 cup sifted confectioners'	1 teaspoon grated
sugar	lemon zest
3/4 cup (1 1/2 sticks) butter	1/4 cup fresh lemon juice
1/2 teaspoon baking powder	Additional confectioners' sugar

Combine 2 cups of the flour and 1/2 cup confectioners' sugar in a bowl. Cut in the butter with a pastry blender or fork until crumbly. Press firmly and evenly in a 9×13-inch baking pan. Bake in a preheated 350-degree oven for 20 to 25 minutes or until brown. Remove from the oven. Maintain the oven temperature.

Mix the remaining 1/2 cup flour and the baking powder together. Combine the eggs, granulated sugar, lemon zest and lemon juice in a bowl and mix well. Stir in the flour mixture. Pour over the prepared crust. Bake for 20 to 25 minutes or until set and light brown. Remove from the oven to cool completely. Cut into squares and dust with additional confectioners' sugar.

Makes 2 dozen

ROASTED STRAWBERRIES WITH LEMON BUTTER COOKIES AND MINT WHIPPED CREAM

ROASTED STRAWBERRIES
32	strawberries, hulled
1/2	cup (1 stick) butter, softened
1/2	cup sugar

LEMON BUTTER COOKIES
1/4	cup all-purpose flour
1/4	cup almond flour
1/2	cup confectioners' sugar
1/2	cup (1 stick) butter, softened

	Zest of 2 lemons
6	tablespoons butter, softened

MINT WHIPPED CREAM
1/4	cup water
1/4	cup sugar
2	cups loosely packed fresh mint leaves
1	cup heavy whipping cream

Fresh mint leaves for garnish

Lemon zest for garnish

To prepare the strawberries, roll the strawberries in the butter and then in the sugar. Place top side down on a baking sheet. Bake in a preheated 350-degree oven for 10 minutes or until the strawberries are soft and begin to release their juices.

To prepare the cookies, combine the all-purpose flour, almond flour, confectioners' sugar, 1/2 cup butter and the lemon zest in a bowl and mix to form a dough. Flatten the dough on a cookie sheet. Bake in a preheated 325-degree oven for 20 minutes or until golden brown. Remove from the oven and maintain the oven temperature. Cool the cookies for 4 minutes. Crumble into fine pieces in a bowl. Add 6 tablespoons butter and mix well. Spread on the cookie sheet. Bake for 8 minutes or until set. Cut into desired shapes while warm. These cookies are fragile. Chill if needed to harden.

To prepare the whipped cream, boil the water and sugar in a saucepan for 3 minutes. Remove from the heat. Stir in the mint. Chill for 1 hour. Strain the syrup, discarding the mint. Whip the mint syrup and whipping cream in a mixing bowl until soft peaks form.

To serve, place the cookies on dessert plates with the strawberries and whipped cream. Pour the juices from the strawberries over each plate. Garnish with mint leaves and lemon zest.

Serves 8

Garden Party

Since 1948, Wilmington has celebrated the arrival of spring through the Azalea Festival, held in early April against the backdrop of blooms of pink, red, purple, and white. This festival came to fruition more than sixty years ago when Dr. W. Houston Moore, active in the Rotary Club, invited local civic club leaders to explore ways to honor the gardens in the area. What began as a simple idea to acknowledge the beautiful flora and fauna has grown to incorporate parties, concerts, and a street fair that collectively attract more than 300,000 people to the area annually.

A parade marks the official beginning of the five-day event and heralds the arrival of Queen Azalea, who is usually a celebrity with local ties. After her coronation, the party begins! The Cape Fear Garden Club sponsors local teenage girls to serve as hostesses in the gardens featured on the popular Garden Tour. Known fondly as "Azalea Belles," these young ladies dressed in antebellum gowns add as much color to the gardens as the flowers themselves. Other fun festival events include a children's tea, a circus, a shag contest, and a juried art show. The place to be and be seen following the Garden Party is Dockside Restaurant and Marina located on Airlie Road overlooking the Intracoastal Waterway. The lively after-party is a perfect way to end a fun-filled day!

Whether you attend the garden party or host your own event to welcome springtime, all Southern belles know that a divine table spread is essential to the perfect celebration.

Let's celebrate

Lucy Lee's

Fiftieth Birthday

with all the girls!

Garden Party

at Airlie

Tuesday, April sixteenth

eleven o'clock

Sarah Jane and Martha

please say yes!

hat and gloves optional

Garden Party

Azalea Punch 48

Honeydew and Lemon Grass Soda Water 48

Seaside Gourgères 49

Vodka-Infused Tomatoes 50

Carolina Crab Dip 50

Spinach Tomato Dip 51

Cream Cheese with Apricot Preserves 51

Cucumber-Watercress Tea Sandwiches 52

Pimento Cheese Sandwiches 53

Rosemary Pimento Cheese Sandwiches 53

White Cheddar Pimento Cheese Sandwiches 54

Devonshire Grapes 54

Chess Squares 55

Chocolate Chip Cake 55

AZALEA PUNCH

1	(64-ounce) bottle cranberry juice cocktail or cran-raspberry juice
1/2	cup sugar or equivalent amount of sugar substitute
1/2	cup lime juice
3	cups citron vodka or raspberry vodka
1/2	cup orange liqueur
1	(1-liter) bottle lemon-lime soda, chilled
2	to 3 oranges, sliced for garnish

Combine the cranberry juice, sugar and lime juice in a large freezer-safe container. Stir in the vodka and liqueur. Freeze, covered, for 4 hours or until slushy. Spoon into a punch bowl. Add the lemon-lime soda just before serving and mix gently. Ladle into martini glasses and garnish each with an orange slice.

To prepare a nonalcoholic version of Azalea Punch, omit the vodka and liqueur. Stir in two pints thawed raspberry sorbet and the soda just before serving.

Serves 16 to 18

HONEYDEW AND LEMON GRASS SODA WATER

1	honeydew melon, cut into balls with a melon baller
3	stalks lemon grass, cut into 4-inch pieces

Juice of 1 lemon

3 3/4 liters club soda

Fresh mint for garnish

Combine the melon balls, lemongrass, lemon juice and club soda in a glass pitcher. Chill for 1 hour. To serve, divide the melon balls into glasses with one piece of lemongrass and add the soda water mixture. Garnish with mint.

Serves 8

SEASIDE GOUGÈRES

1	cup water
1/2	cup (1 stick) butter
1	cup all-purpose flour
4	eggs
3	scallions, chopped
1	teaspoon dry mustard
1	teaspoon white wine Worcestershire sauce
3/4	cup (3 ounces) shredded Gruyère cheese
8	ounces fresh lump crab meat, shells removed and meat flaked, or
	1 (6-ounce) can crab meat, drained and flaked

Bring the water and butter to a boil in a saucepan. Remove immediately from the heat. Add the flour. Beat with a wooden spoon for 1 minute or until the pastry is smooth and forms a ball. Beat in the eggs one at a time. Stir in the scallions, dry mustard, Worcestershire sauce and cheese. Fold in the crab meat. Drop the dough by tablespoonfuls onto a parchment-lined baking sheet. Bake in a preheated 400-degree oven for 15 minutes. Reduce the oven temperature to 350 degrees. Bake for 10 to 15 minutes longer or until puffed and golden brown. Cool slightly before removing from the baking sheet. Serve warm as an appetizer or as an accompaniment to soup or salad.

Makes 2 dozen

VODKA-INFUSED TOMATOES

> 1   pint cherry tomatoes or grape tomatoes
> Vodka
> 2   tablespoons sea salt, or to taste
> 1   tablespoon lemon pepper, or to taste

Poke the tomatoes five or six times with a wooden pick or skewer and place in a sealable plastic bag. Pour enough vodka into the bag to cover the tomatoes and seal the bag. Let stand at room temperature for 8 to 10 hours. Mix the sea salt and lemon pepper in a small bowl. Serve the tomatoes with the dipping salt on the side.

Serves 8 to 10

CAROLINA CRAB DIP

> 8   ounces low-fat or regular cream cheese, softened
> 1   (16-ounce) can back-fin crab meat, chilled and meat flaked
> 1   (12-ounce) jar cocktail sauce, chilled
> 1   to 2 teaspoons horseradish
> Old Bay seasoning to taste
> Pepper to taste

Spread the cream cheese over the entire surface of a large serving plate. Sprinkle the crab meat evenly over the cream cheese. Spread the cocktail sauce and horseradish evenly over the crab meat. Sprinkle with Old Bay seasoning and pepper. Serve immediately with assorted crackers or crostini.

Serves 8

SPINACH TOMATO DIP

1	large bag fresh spinach
Olive oil	
24	ounces cream cheese, softened
1	teaspoon minced garlic
1	(4-ounce) can jalapeño chiles
2	tomatoes, coarsely chopped
Salt and pepper to taste	
2	cups (8 ounces) shredded Monterey Jack and Cheddar cheese

Sauté the spinach in olive oil in a skillet until wilted. Combine with the cream cheese in a bowl and mix well. Add the garlic, jalapeño chiles, tomatoes, salt and pepper and mix well. Spread in a baking dish. Sprinkle with the Monterey Jack and Cheddar cheese. Bake in a preheated 350-degree oven for 30 minutes or until bubbly on top. Serve with assorted crackers or crostini.

Serves 12

CREAM CHEESE WITH APRICOT PRESERVES

8	ounces cream cheese
1/2	cup apricot preserves
4	scallions, chopped

Place the cream cheese on a serving platter. Spread the preserves over the cream cheese. Sprinkle with the scallions. Serve with thin wheat crackers.

Serves 12

CUCUMBER-WATERCRESS TEA SANDWICHES

8	ounces cream cheese, softened
3/4	cup finely chopped or grated cucumber
2	teaspoons minced fresh watercress
1	teaspoon fresh lemon juice

Dash of Worcestershire sauce

1/4	teaspoon seasoned salt
1/4	teaspoon cayenne pepper
24	slices whole wheat bread
1	cup fresh watercress, trimmed and minced
6	tablespoons butter, softened

Beat the cream cheese, cucumber, 2 teaspoons watercress, the lemon juice, Worcestershire sauce, seasoned salt and cayenne pepper in a mixing bowl until smooth or process in a food processor. Cut two circles from each bread slice with a 2-inch round cutter. Spread the cucumber mixture evenly on one-half of the bread circles. Top with the remaining bread circles.

Place 1 cup watercress onto a plate or cutting board. Spread the outer edge of each sandwich with some of the butter. Roll the edge of each sandwich in the watercress, pressing very lightly to coat. Cover with a very slightly damp cloth. Chill for 1 hour or longer.

Makes 2 dozen tea sandwiches

PIMENTO CHEESE SANDWICHES

4   ounces extra-sharp white or yellow Cheddar cheese, shredded

1   (2-ounce) jar pimento, drained and finely chopped

2   tablespoons mayonnaise

1/2   teaspoon hot pepper sauce

Salt to taste

4   slices whole wheat bread

4   thin slices sweet onion (optional)

1   cup watercress sprigs, trimmed

Mash the cheese, pimento, mayonnaise and hot sauce in a small bowl with a fork until well mixed. Add salt and mix well. Chill, covered, for 1 hour to meld the flavors. Spread on one-half of the bread slices. Top with the onion slices and watercress. Top with the remaining bread slices. Cut each sandwich into halves and serve.

Makes 2 sandwiches

ROSEMARY PIMENTO CHEESE SANDWICHES

10   ounces sharp Cheddar cheese

10   ounces extra-sharp Cheddar cheese

3/4   cup mayonnaise

2   sprigs of fresh rosemary

1   teaspoon finely grated onion

1   garlic clove, minced

Salt and black pepper to taste

Dash of Worcestershire sauce

Red pepper flakes to taste

4   (4-ounce) jars pimentos, drained and finely chopped

12   to 16 slices white or wheat bread

Process the cheese in a food processor until finely shedded. Add the mayonnaise and mix well. Add the rosemary, onion, garlic, salt, black pepper, Worcestershire sauce, red pepper flakes and pimentos and process well. Spread on one-half of the bread slices. Top with the remaining bread slices. Cut into halves and serve.

Makes 6 to 8 sandwiches

WHITE CHEDDAR PIMENTO CHEESE SANDWICHES

8   cups (2 pounds) shredded white Cheddar cheese
1   (4-ounce) jar pimentos, drained and chopped
1 1/2   tablespoons sweet relish
2   cups mayonnaise
12   to 16 slices sourdough bread

Combine the cheese, pimentos, relish and mayonnaise in a bowl and mix well. Spread on one-half of the bread slices. Top with the remaining bread slices.

Makes 6 to 8 sandwiches

DEVONSHIRE GRAPES

2   pounds seedless green grapes
2   pounds seedless red grapes
8   ounces cream cheese, softened
1   cup sour cream
1/2   cup granulated sugar
1   teaspoon vanilla extract
4   ounces pecans, lightly toasted and chopped
2   tablespoons light brown sugar

Rinse the grapes and remove from the stems. Dry the grapes thoroughly. Beat the cream cheese, sour cream, granulated sugar and vanilla in a bowl until smooth. Fold in the grapes by hand. Chill, covered, for 3 to 24 hours before serving. Sprinkle with the pecans and brown sugar and mix until evenly distributed.

Serves 8 to 10

CHESS SQUARES

1	(2-layer) package yellow cake mix
1/2	cup (1 stick) butter, softened
1	egg
8	ounces cream cheese, softened
1	(1-pound) package confectioners' sugar
3	eggs

Combine the cake mix, butter and one egg in a bowl and mix well. Press over the bottom of a 9×13-inch baking pan. Combine the cream cheese, confectioners' sugar and three eggs in a bowl and mix well. Pour over the cake mix mixture. Bake in a preheated 350-degree oven for 45 minutes. Remove from the oven and cool completely. Cut into squares.

Makes 2 dozen

CHOCOLATE CHIP CAKE

1	(2-layer) package yellow cake mix
1	(3-ounce) package vanilla instant pudding mix
2	cups (12 ounces) semisweet chocolate chips
12	ounces pecans, coarsely chopped
4	eggs
1	cup sour cream
2/3	cup vegetable oil

Combine the cake mix, pudding mix, chocolate chips and pecans in a bowl. Stir in the eggs, sour cream and oil. Spoon into a bundt pan sprayed generously with nonstick baking spray. Bake in a preheated 325-degree oven for 1 hour. Cool in the pan for 5 minutes. Invert onto a wire rack to cool completely.

Serves 16

Porch Parties

Porch parties are held in the late afternoon under the wide porch overhang that shades all from the summer rays while harnessing the pleasant cool breezes off the river and ocean waters. Southerners long ago embraced the architectural advantages of porches, making them a tasteful feature found among the historic homes of Wilmington. At the turn of the century Wilmington was known for its skilled iron-works artisans, who adorned local porches and gardens with unique gates and trellises. Much time was spent on the porch, where spontaneous and planned parties became part of the rich Southern tradition, sometimes spilling out onto the front lawns on lovely May evenings.

Never missing an opportunity to celebrate our heritage or to take time to visit with friends and family, a porch party is a wonderful way to entertain in a very Southern way. With the broad and spacious porches of the 1849 mansion of Poplar Grove Plantation as a backdrop, the Junior League of Wilmington celebrates the warmth of May with a Mint Julep Jubilee. Ladies mix and mingle under beautiful wide-brimmed hats decorated with bows, flowers, and feathers. Frozen Margarita Punch, Cape Fear Crab Cakes, Baked Shrimp and Artichoke Dip, and Beach Cottage Pie are musts for a carefree evening laughing with friends. The Kentucky Derby is the culminating event of a lovely Southern evening on the lawn beyond the porches!

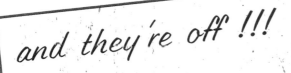

and they're off !!!

Please join the
Junior League of Wilmington
for mint juleps & southern fare

*Mint Julep
Jubilee*

Saturday, May 1
3-8 p.m.
Poplar Grove Plantation

Kentucky Derby
attire

Reservations
910-799-7405

Proceeds benefit community programs of JLW

Porch Parties

Jubilee Julep   60

Frozen Margarita Punch   60

Baked Shrimp and Artichoke Dip   61

Seven-Layer Shrimp Dip   61

Pineapple Cheese Ball   62

Riverwalk Salad   62

Roasted Vegetable Salad   63

Cape Fear Crab Cakes   64

Rémoulade Sauce   64

Braised Pork Tenderloin   65

Grilled Fruit Kabobs   66

Beach Cottage Pie   66

Easy Key Lime Pie   67

JUBILEE JULEP

1	cup water
1	cup granulated sugar
2	bunches fresh mint leaves

Bourbon
Mint leaves for garnish
Confectioners' sugar, optional

Combine the water, granulated sugar and 1 bunch of the mint leaves in a small saucepan over high heat. Bring to a boil and boil for 5 minutes or until the sugar is dissolved. Allow to cool for about 1 hour. Refrigerate overnight in a jar. Pour through a strainer to remove the mint leaves.

For each serving, muddle a few mint leaves from the remaining 1 bunch of mint leaves in the bottom of a frozen glass or silver mint julep cup. Fill the glass with crushed ice. Pour 2 tablespoons of the mint syrup and 1/4 cup bourbon over the ice. Garnish with a mint leaf and sprinkle with confectioners' sugar. Serve with a straw that has been trimmed to just 1 inch above the top of the cup.

Serves 10

FROZEN MARGARITA PUNCH

4	(12-ounce) cans frozen limeade concentrate, thawed
3	quarts (12 cups) water
3	cups tequila
3	cups Triple Sec
2	(2-liter) bottles lemon-lime soda, chilled

Lime slices for garnish

Combine the limeade concentrate, water, tequila and Triple Sec in a large freezer container. Freeze for 8 hours or longer. Remove from the freezer and let stand for 30 minutes before serving. Spoon into glasses. Add the lemon-lime soda and stir until slushy. Garnish with lime slices.

Makes 2 1/2 gallons

BAKED SHRIMP AND ARTICHOKE DIP

1/2 cup (2 ounces) shredded Cheddar cheese

1/2 cup (2 ounces) shredded mozzarella cheese

1 cup (4 ounces) grated Parmesan cheese

1 (14-ounce) can artichoke hearts, drained and chopped

1/2 cup chopped onion

1/2 teaspoon garlic salt

1/2 cup mayonnaise

1 cup peeled cooked shrimp

Dash of paprika for garnish

Mix the Cheddar cheese, mozzarella cheese and Parmesan cheese in a
bowl. Add the artichoke hearts, onion, garlic salt, mayonnaise and shrimp and
mix well. Spoon into a medium baking dish. Sprinkle with paprika. Bake in a
preheated 350-degree oven for 20 minutes or until bubbly and light brown. Serve
with toasted baguette slices.

Serves 20

SEVEN-LAYER SHRIMP DIP

8 ounces cream cheese, softened

1/4 cup heavy cream

1/2 (12-ounce) bottle chili sauce

4 ounces cooked salad shrimp, drained

6 scallions, chopped

3/4 cup chopped green bell pepper

1 (3-ounce) can pitted black olives, sliced

2 cups (8 ounces) shredded mozzarella cheese

Combine the cream cheese and cream in a bowl and mix until smooth.
Spread evenly in a 9×13-inch serving dish. Layer the chili sauce, shrimp, scallions,
bell pepper, olives and mozzarella cheese in the order listed over the cream cheese
mixture. Chill for 1 hour before serving. Serve with tortilla chips.

Serves 8 to 10

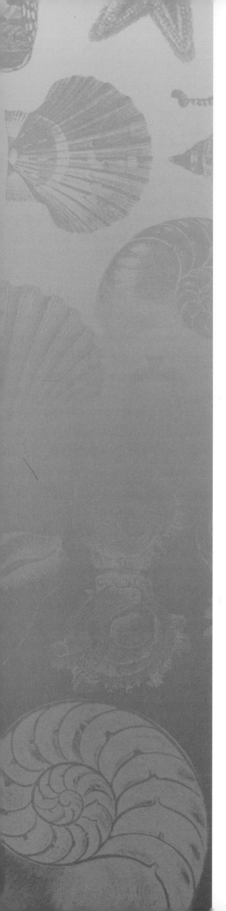

PINEAPPLE CHEESE BALL

16 ounces cream cheese, softened
1 (8-ounce) can crushed pineapple, drained
1/4 cup chopped green bell pepper
2 tablespoons finely chopped onion
1 tablespoon seasoned salt
Garlic powder to taste
2 cups chopped pecans

Mix the cream cheese, pineapple, bell pepper, onion, seasoned salt, garlic powder and 1 cup of the pecans in a bowl. Shape into a ball and roll in the remaining 1 cup pecans. Wrap tightly in plastic wrap and store in the refrigerator. Serve with crackers.

Serves 20

RIVERWALK SALAD

1 cup vegetable oil
1/2 cup red wine vinegar
2 tablespoons soy sauce
1/2 cup sugar
2 (3-ounce) packages ramen noodles, crumbled
1/4 cup sesame seeds
3/4 cup almonds
1/4 cup (1/2 stick) butter, melted
2 heads romaine, chopped
1 bunch green onions, chopped

Mix the oil, vinegar, soy sauce and sugar in an airtight container. Chill, covered, for 8 to 10 hours. Shake and bring to room temperature before serving. Discard the seasoning packets from the ramen noodles or save for another use. Combine the ramen noodles, sesame seeds, almonds and butter in a bowl and toss to mix. Spread on a baking sheet.

Bake in a preheated 375-degree oven for 6 to 8 minutes or until brown, watching carefully to prevent overbrowning. Toss the lettuce and green onions with the vinaigrette in a salad bowl to coat. Add the ramen noodle mixture just before serving.

Serves 10 to 12

ROASTED VEGETABLE SALAD

2	large eggplant
2	large zucchini
2	yellow squash
2	cups chopped onion
1/2	cup olive oil
1	tablespoon salt

Pepper to taste

1	cup finely chopped assorted fresh herbs, such as chives, tarragon, dill weed, chervil, basil, cilantro and/or parsley
1/4	tablespoon olive oil
2	tablespoons lemon juice
1	tablespoon chopped garlic

Salt to taste

8	ounces feta cheese, crumbled (optional)

Peel the eggplant and cut into 1/2-inch pieces. Cut the zucchini and squash into 1/2-inch pieces. Combine the eggplant, zucchini, squash, onion, 1/2 cup olive oil, 1 tablespoon salt and pepper in a large bowl and toss to evenly coat. Spread in a single layer in a large roasting pan.

Roast in a preheated 350-degree oven for 45 minutes. Remove from the oven and let cool for 15 minutes. Place the roasted vegetables in a large bowl. Add the herbs, 1/4 tablespoon olive oil, the lemon juice, garlic, salt to taste and pepper and toss to coat. Add the cheese and toss to mix.

Serves 8

Cape Fear Crab Cakes

2	eggs
1	tablespoon mayonnaise
2	teaspoons Worcestershire sauce
1	teaspoon Old Bay seasoning
1	teaspoon dry mustard
1/4	teaspoon white pepper
1	pound Maryland crab meat, shells removed and meat flaked
1/2	cup saltine cracker crumbs

Vegetable oil for deep-frying

Combine the eggs, mayonnaise, Worcestershire sauce, Old Bay seasoning, dry mustard and white pepper in a bowl and mix well. Add the crab meat and mix gently. Add the cracker crumbs and mix to evenly distribute through the mixture. Shape into six patties. Chill for 2 hours. Deep-fry in preheated 350-degree oil in a deep fryer for 2 to 3 minutes or until golden brown. Drain on paper towels. Serve with Rémoulade Sauce (below).

Note: The crab patties can be sautéed in a small amount of oil in a skillet for 5 minutes on each side, or broiled on a rack in a broiler pan for 10 minutes on each side.

Serves 6

Rémoulade Sauce

1/2	cup mayonnaise
1/2	cup nonfat yogurt
4	green onions, finely chopped
2	tablespoons Creole mustard
2	teaspoons minced garlic
1/4	teaspoon ground red pepper

Combine the mayonnaise, yogurt, green onions, Creole mustard, garlic and red pepper in a bowl and mix well. Chill, covered, until serving time.

Serves 10

BRAISED PORK TENDERLOIN

3   pounds pork tenderloin

5   to 6 tablespoons extra-virgin olive oil

Salt and pepper to taste

1/4   cup (1/2 stick) butter

1   large shallot, coarsely chopped

1   small onion, coarsely chopped

1   cup button mushrooms, coarsely chopped

2   ribs celery, coarsely chopped

1   carrot, coarsely chopped

2   garlic cloves, minced

2   cups dry white wine

2   bay leaves

1   tablespoon poultry seasoning

1/2   teaspoon ground cumin

4   cups (about) chicken stock

2   tablespoons all-purpose flour

Remove the pork from the refrigerator and let stand at room temperature for a few minutes. Tie with butcher's twine in three places to prevent falling apart while cooking. Drizzle with 1 to 2 tablespoons of the olive oil to lightly coat. Sprinkle with salt and pepper on all sides.

Heat 2 tablespoons of the remaining olive oil and 2 tablespoons of the butter in a Dutch oven or large stockpot over medium to high heat. Add the shallot, onion, mushrooms, celery and carrot. Cook until the vegetables are tender. Add the garlic. Cook for 1 to 2 minutes. Add the wine. Cook for 1 to 2 minutes, stirring to deglaze the bottom of the Dutch oven. Remove the vegetable mixture from the Dutch oven.

Add the remaining 2 tablespoons olive oil and 2 tablespoons butter to the Dutch oven. Heat over medium to high heat until the butter melts. Add the pork. Cook until the pork is brown and releases from the bottom of the Dutch oven. Repeat the process on all sides until brown all over but not cooked through. Reduce the heat to medium. Return the vegetable mixture to the Dutch oven. Add the bay leaves, poultry seasoning and cumin. Add enough stock to cover the vegetables and at least the bottom third of the pork. Sprinkle with salt and pepper. Simmer, covered, until the pork is cooked through, turning every 30 minutes. Discard the bay leaves before serving.

Serves 6

GRILLED FRUIT KABOBS

3	peaches
4	plums
3	star fruit
4	kiwifruit
1	pineapple

Soak wooden skewers in water for 30 minutes. Cut the peaches, plums, star fruit and kiwifruit into 1/2-inch slices. Cut the pineapple into 1/2×2-inch chunks. All of the pineapple will not be needed. Thread the fruit alternately onto each skewer. Place on a grill rack. Grill over medium heat for 2 to 3 minutes on each side or until warm. Serve with ice cream or whipped cream, if desired.

Serves 8

BEACH COTTAGE PIE

24	ounces cottage cheese
5	eggs
3/4	cup sugar
1	teaspoon vanilla extract
1	teaspoon salt
13/4	cups milk
2	unbaked (9-inch) pie shells
Cinnamon to taste	

Process the cottage cheese in a blender until smooth. Add the eggs and sugar and blend well. Add the vanilla, salt and milk and blend well. Pour into the pie shells. Sprinkle lightly with cinnamon. Bake in a preheated 375-degree oven for 20 minutes. Reduce the oven temperature to 350 degrees. Bake for 35 minutes longer or until set and a knife inserted in the center comes out clean.

Serves 16

Easy Key Lime Pie

1   (14-ounce) can sweetened condensed milk

4   egg yolks

3/4   cup fresh lime juice

1   (9-inch) graham cracker pie shell

1   cup whipping cream

Sugar to taste

Pour the condensed milk into a bowl. Add the egg yolks one at a time, beating well after each addition. Add the lime juice gradually, beating constantly until blended. Pour into the pie shell. Bake in a preheated 350-degree oven for 10 minutes. Remove to a wire rack to cool completely.

Beat the whipping cream in a bowl until soft peaks form. Add the sugar and mix well. Spread over the cooled pie. Cut into wedges to serve.

Serves 8 to 10

Boxed Lunch at the Beach

Boating enthusiasts abound in Wilmington. Their destinations are often the numerous sandbars and islands that populate the waters between the Atlantic Ocean and the Intracoastal Waterway. Masonboro Island proves to be one of the most popular mooring sites, if typical weekends between May and September serve as any indication. The north end of the island closest to Wrightsville Beach is a great spot for "tying up" boats for the day and lounging on the sand, letting the kids and the dogs run free.

The area beaches offer other options for people to get out on the water: surfing, sailing, kayaking, and paddleboarding are popular activities among outdoor enthusiasts from Figure Eight Island to Kure Beach. Crystal Pier, which houses the Oceanic Restaurant, is a popular spot for surfers. Between Harbor Island and Wrightsville Beach, many enjoy sailing a Sunfish, kayaking in Banks Channel, or paddleboarding around the marshes. For land lovers, a leisurely cruise down the beach on a bike is the ideal way to pedal away an afternoon. The North Carolina Aquarium at Fort Fisher on Pleasure Island is a spectacular place to visit when the sun is *not* shining!

Beachgoing, whether in the water or on land, can work up an appetite! A picnic lunch on the sand will reinvigorate a tired soul. Fill your baskets with pimento cheese and chicken salad sandwiches, crisp pickles, and Pasta Salad. Wash it all down with Mint Iced Tea and top it off with Beach Brownies for dessert—delicious!

Bring your kids & puppy dogs too
We can't wait to party with you.
A box lunch to feed your crowd
Swimsuits are definitely allowed!

MASONBORO ISLAND FUN

Sunday, June 25th
4-7 pm

Sue & Sam

Miss the boat?
Call 910-888-8888

Boxed Lunch
at the
Beach

Mint Iced Tea   72

Cheese Crispies   72

Black Bean Dip   73

Curried Chicken Salad   73

Jalapeño Pimento Cheese   74

Roasted Red Pepper and Prosciutto Sandwiches   75

Picnic Slaw   75

Pasta Salad   76

Refrigerator Pickles   76

Beach Brownies   77

Cherry Chocolate Oatmeal Cookies   77

MINT ICED TEA

13   tea bags

1/4   cup lightly packed fresh mint leaves

2   cups water

Juice from 2 lemons

1   (6-ounce) can frozen orange juice concentrate

1   cup sugar

Sprigs of fresh mint for garnish

Combine the tea bags, 1/4 cup mint leaves and the water in a large saucepan. Cover and bring to a boil. Remove immediately from the heat. Steep for 30 minutes. Add the lemon juice, orange juice concentrate and sugar and mix well. Add enough water to measure 2 quarts. Strain into a pitcher, discarding the solids. Chill in the refrigerator until serving time. Pour into glasses and garnish with sprigs of fresh mint.

Serves 12

CHEESE CRISPIES

1   cup (2 sticks) butter, softened

8   ounces extra-sharp Cheddar cheese, shredded

1 2/3 cups all-purpose flour

1/4   teaspoon salt

1/2   teaspoon cayenne pepper

3 1/2 cups crisp rice cereal

Combine the butter and cheese in a bowl and mix well. Add the flour, salt and cayenne pepper gradually and mix well. Add the cereal and mix well. Shape into balls. Place on an ungreased baking sheet and flatten with a fork. Bake in a preheated 325-degree oven for 12 to 15 minutes or until light golden brown.

Makes 5 dozen

BLACK BEAN DIP

1	(11-ounce) can white Shoe Peg corn
1	(15-ounce) can black beans, drained and rinsed
1	(10-ounce) can mild tomatoes with green chiles, drained
1	envelope taco seasoning mix
1	tablespoon mayonnaise
1/2	cup chopped fresh cilantro

Combine the corn, beans, tomatoes with green chiles, taco seasoning mix, mayonnaise and cilantro in a bowl and mix well. Chill until serving time. Serve with tortilla chips.

Serves 6 to 8

CURRIED CHICKEN SALAD

3/4	cup mayonnaise
1	tablespoon lemon juice
1/8	teaspoon curry powder
1/8	teaspoon garlic powder
1	teaspoon soy sauce
2	cups chopped cooked chicken
1	(10-ounce) package frozen green peas, cooked and drained
1	cup chopped celery
1	onion, minced
1/2	cup sliced almonds
1	(3-ounce) can chow mein noodles
	Lettuce leaves

Blend the mayonnaise, lemon juice, curry powder, garlic powder and soy sauce in a bowl. Combine the chicken, peas, celery and onion in a bowl and mix well. Stir in the mayonnaise mixture. Chill for 1 hour. Stir in the almonds and chow mein noodles just before serving. Serve on lettuce-lined salad plates.

Serves 6

JALAPEÑO PIMENTO CHEESE

8	ounces extra-extra-sharp Cheddar cheese
8	ounces extra-sharp Cheddar cheese
1	(2-ounce) jar chopped pimento
2	tablespoons diced pickled jalapeño chiles, seeds removed
1/4	cup pickled jalapeño chile juice
3	dashes of Worcestershire sauce
50	grinds of black pepper, or to taste
4	tablespoons (rounded) light mayonnaise

Remove the cheese from the refrigerator and let stand for 1 to 2 hours. Shred the cheese into a large mixing bowl. Add the pimento, jalapeño chiles, jalapeño chile juice, Worcestershire sauce, pepper and mayonnaise and mix with a fork. Do not overmix. The mixture should be lumpy. Chill in the refrigerator. Remove from the refrigerator and let stand for 20 minutes before serving. Serve with crackers.

Note: Do not let the cheese become too warm before shredding or it will crumble, making a smooth pimento cheese. This recipe is best with more texture and lumps. Because it does not have a creamy base and has a bite to it, it is best served with crackers rather than as a sandwich spread. The flavor of this pimento cheese is dependant upon using an extra-sharp Cheddar cheese. Because this spread is spicy and the jalapeño chiles make it akin to a Mexican spread, a cold robust beer is a nice complement to its flavor.

Makes about 1 pound

ROASTED RED PEPPER AND PROSCIUTTO SANDWICHES

1	loaf focaccia	1	(16-ounce) jar roasted
1/2	cup goat cheese		red peppers, drained
8	ounces thinly sliced		and chopped
	prosciutto	1 1/2	cups arugula
		1/2	cup olive tapenade or
			pesto

Cut the bread horizontally into halves. Spread the goat cheese on the cut side of one-half of the bread. Layer the prosciutto, red peppers and arugula over the goat cheese. Spread the tapenade on the cut side of the remaining bread. Replace the bread half tapenade side down to form a sandwich. Cut into four sections.

Serves 4

PICNIC SLAW

1	head cabbage, shredded	2	tablespoons sugar
1	carrot, shredded	1	tablespoon Dijon
1/2	cup chopped onion		mustard
1/2	cup chopped celery	1	teaspoon salt
1/4	cup chopped green	1/2	teaspoon paprika
	bell pepper	1/2	teaspoon pepper
1/2	cup sour cream	1/2	teaspoon celery seeds
1/2	cup mayonnaise		
2	tablespoons apple		
	cider vinegar		

Combine the cabbage, carrot, onion, celery and bell pepper in a bowl and toss to mix. Mix the sour cream, mayonnaise, vinegar, sugar, Dijon mustard, salt, paprika, pepper and celery seeds in a bowl. Pour over the vegetables and toss gently to coat. Chill, covered, until serving time.

Serves 6 to 8

PASTA SALAD

1	(12-ounce) bottle poppy seed salad dressing	1	cup finely chopped carrots
1	(12-ounce) bottle Italian salad dressing	2	tomatoes, finely chopped
1	envelope Italian salad dressing mix	1/2	cup finely chopped red bell pepper
24	ounces pasta, cooked and drained	1/2	cup finely chopped yellow bell pepper
2	cups chopped ham	1/2	cup finely chopped green bell pepper
1	cup finely chopped celery	2	cucumbers, finely chopped

Mix the poppy seed salad dressing, Italian salad dressing and salad dressing mix in a large bowl. Add the pasta, ham, celery, carrots, tomatoes, bell peppers and cucumbers and mix well. Chill, covered, until serving time.

Serves 6 to 8

REFRIGERATOR PICKLES

2	pounds Kirby pickling cucumbers	1/2	teaspoon mustard seeds
1	large onion, thinly sliced	1/2	teaspoon celery seeds
1 1/2	cups white wine vinegar	1/2	teaspoon turmeric
3/4	cup sugar	3/4	teaspoon crushed red pepper
4	teaspoons minced garlic	1/4	teaspoon freshly cracked black pepper
1	teaspoon salt		

Layer the cucumbers and onion one-half at a time in a glass baking dish or plastic container. Combine the vinegar, sugar, garlic, salt, mustard seeds, celery seeds, turmeric, red pepper and black pepper in a small saucepan and mix well. Bring to a boil. Boil for 1 minute. Pour over the cucumber and onion layers. Let stand until cool. Chill, covered, for 3 to 4 days before serving. The pickles can be stored in the refrigerator for 1 month.

Serves 10 to 12

BEACH BROWNIES

1/2	cup sugar	2	eggs
1/3	cup butter	3/4	cup all-purpose flour
2	tablespoons water	1/4	teaspoon baking soda
1	teaspoon vanilla extract	1/4	teaspoon salt
1	cup (6 ounces) semisweet chocolate chips	1	cup pecans or walnuts, chopped (optional)

Bring the sugar, butter and water to a boil in a saucepan over high heat, stirring constantly. Remove from the heat. Add the vanilla and chocolate chips and stir until smooth. Let stand until slightly cool. Stir in the eggs one at a time. Add a mixture of the flour, baking soda and salt and mix well. Stir in the pecans. Pour into a greased 9×9-inch baking pan. Bake in a preheated 325-degree oven for 30 minutes. Remove from the oven to cool. Cut into squares.

Makes 1 1/2 dozen

CHERRY CHOCOLATE OATMEAL COOKIES

1 1/2	cups all-purpose flour	1/2	cup granulated sugar
1	teaspoon baking powder	2	eggs
2	cups rolled oats	1 1/2	teaspoons vanilla extract
1	cup (2 sticks) butter, softened	2	cups dried cherries
1	cup packed brown sugar	1	cup (6 ounces) dark chocolate chips

Mix the flour, baking powder and oats together. Cream the butter, brown sugar and granulated sugar in a mixing bowl until light and fluffy. Add the eggs and vanilla and mix well. Add the oat mixture and mix well. Stir in the dried cherries and chocolate chips. Drop by rounded tablespoonfuls onto a cookie sheet. Bake in a preheated 350-degree oven for 10 to 12 minutes or until golden brown. Cool on the cookie sheet for 5 minutes. Remove to a wire rack to cool completely.

Makes 2 dozen

4th of July
by the
Water

The pinnacle of summer, Independence Day, is best celebrated by the water. In the coastal area of southeastern North Carolina, there are many options, including the Cape Fear River, the Atlantic Ocean, the Intracoastal Waterway, and the plethora of sounds and inlets among the barrier islands. You could set out on a bike for a ride along the river to sea path or take your bicycles across the river on the Fort Fisher ferry to historic Southport for the official North Carolina 4th of July Festival, complete with parade and street fair. Preserved natural beauty is just another ferry ride away over to Bald Head Island, where no cars are allowed, but golf carts will be adorned in their finest red, white, and blue for the holiday. If you prefer to relax with a good summer book by the ocean shore, you can sit back with a tall glass of refreshing Basil-Infused Watermelon Lemonade while waiting for the evening full of colorful skies. Amazing firework shows and delicious food will be the foundation of memories and friendships year after year. Picnic baskets full of scrumptious goodies such as Old Baldy Pasta Salad, Chicken Burgers, and Blueberry Cobbler will ensure that everyone enjoys a good old-fashioned outdoor feast. It's a great day to declare "independence" from all things work-related—after the cooking is done!

BRING YOUR FAMILY TO AN

OLD FASHIONED PICNIC AT BALD HEAD ISLAND

Annual Benefit for League Projects

Saturday, July 4th

10-5 pm

FOOD...FUN...FRIENDS

reservations suggested by June 25th–JLW headquarters

4th of July
by the
Water

Basil-Infused Watermelon Lemonade 82

Summer Bean Dip 82

Spicy Deviled Eggs 83

Bacon Cheddar Deviled Eggs 83

Sweet-and-Savory Slider Burgers 84

Chicken Burgers 84

Buttermilk Fried Chicken 85

Grilled Corn and Crab Salad 85

Old Baldy Pasta Salad 86

Broccoli Salad 86

Blueberry Cobbler 87

Peach Crisp 87

BASIL-INFUSED WATERMELON LEMONADE

3/4   cup water

1/2   cup sugar

1   cup loosely packed chopped basil

6   cups chopped seedless watermelon

Juice from 2 lemons

Bring the water and sugar to a boil in a small saucepan. Reduce the heat to low and simmer until the sugar dissolves. Remove from the heat. Add the basil. Chill in the refrigerator. Process the watermelon in a blender until smooth. Strain through a fine strainer into a pitcher, discarding the solids. Stir in the basil mixture and lemon juice. Chill until serving time.

Serves 6 to 8

SUMMER BEAN DIP

8   ounces whipped cream cheese

1   (15-ounce) can black beans, drained and rinsed

1   (16-ounce) jar peach salsa

2   cups (8 ounces) shredded sharp Cheddar cheese

Mix the cream cheese and beans in a bowl. Spread in an 8×8-inch baking dish. Layer the salsa and Cheddar cheese over the top. Bake in a preheated 350-degree oven for 30 minutes or until the cheese is bubbly. Serve with tortilla chips.

Serves 8

SPICY DEVILED EGGS

12	eggs
5	tablespoons light mayonnaise
3	tablespoons minced pickled jalapeño chiles
1	tablespoon mustard
1/2	teaspoon ground cumin
1/2	teaspoon salt
Cilantro for garnish

Place the eggs in a saucepan and cover with cold water. Bring to a boil and remove immediately from the heat. Cover and let stand for 10 to 12 minutes. Remove the eggs from the water and let stand until cool or rinse under cold running water. Peel the eggs and cut into halves lengthwise. Mash the egg yolks in a bowl. Add the mayonnaise, jalapeño chiles, mustard, cumin and salt and mix well. Spoon into a large sealable plastic bag. Cut off a small piece from the corner of the bag. Pipe the egg yolk mixture into the egg whites. Place on a serving plate. Chill, covered, until serving time. Garnish with cilantro.

Serves 12

BACON CHEDDAR DEVILED EGGS

12	eggs
4	slices bacon
1/2	cup mayonnaise
2	tablespoons finely shredded Cheddar cheese
1	tablespoon mustard

Place the eggs in a saucepan and cover with cold water. Bring to a boil and remove immediately from the heat. Cover and let stand for 10 to 12 minutes. Remove the eggs from the water and let stand until cool or rinse under cold running water. Fry the bacon in a large deep skillet over medium-high heat until evenly brown and crisp. Remove the bacon to paper towels to drain. Crumble the bacon. Peel the eggs and cut into halves lengthwise. Mash the egg yolks in a bowl. Add the bacon, mayonnaise and cheese and mix well. Stir in the mustard. Spoon into the egg whites and place on a serving plate. Chill, covered, until serving time.

Serves 12

SWEET-AND-SAVORY SLIDER BURGERS

1/4	cup soy sauce
2	tablespoons corn syrup
1	tablespoon lemon juice
1/2	teaspoon ground ginger
1/4	teaspoon garlic powder
2	green onions, thinly sliced
2	pounds ground beef
1/4	cup chili sauce
1/4	cup jalapeño jelly
8	hamburger buns

Mix the soy sauce, corn syrup, lemon juice, ginger, garlic powder and green onions in a medium bowl. Pour into a shallow baking pan or baking dish. Shape the ground beef into eight patties. Place in a single layer in the marinade, turning to coat each side. Chill, covered, for 4 hours. Drain the patties, reserving the marinade. Place the patties on a grill rack. Grill over medium-high heat for 5 minutes on each side or until cooked through, brushing several times with the reserved marinade. Mix the chili sauce and jelly in a bowl. Serve the patties on the buns with the chili sauce mixture and any desired toppings.

Serves 8

CHICKEN BURGERS

1	pound ground chicken
1 1/2	cups fresh baby spinach, chopped
4	ounces garlic and herb feta cheese, crumbled
2	teaspoons cracked pepper
4	hamburger buns

Combine the chicken, spinach, cheese and pepper in a bowl and mix well. Shape into four patties and place on a grill rack. Grill over medium-high heat for 7 to 10 minutes on each side or until cooked through.

Serves 4

BUTTERMILK FRIED CHICKEN

1	cup buttermilk	2	teaspoons pepper
1	teaspoon salt	1	teaspoon paprika
1/2	teaspoon pepper	1/2	teaspoon poultry
3	pounds chicken, cut up		seasoning
1	cup all-purpose flour	1/2	teaspoon garlic powder
1	teaspoon salt	11/2	cups vegetable oil

Combine the buttermilk, 1 teaspoon salt and 1/2 teaspoon pepper in a bowl. Add the chicken. Chill, covered, for 3 to 10 hours. Mix the flour, 1 teaspoon salt, 2 teaspoons pepper, the paprika, poultry seasoning and garlic powder in a large sealable plastic bag. Drain the chicken, discarding the buttermilk mixture. Place the chicken in the flour mixture and shake to coat. Fry the chicken in preheated 350-degree oil in a large skillet for 15 to 20 minutes or until brown and cooked through, turning once. Drain on paper towels.

Note: You may remove the skin from the chicken before preparing, if desired.

Serves 4 to 6

GRILLED CORN AND CRAB SALAD

4	or 5 ears of summer corn, grilled	1	cup fresh basil, chopped
2	pounds small red potatoes	11/2	pounds fresh crab meat, shells removed and
2	cups cherry tomatoes		meat flaked
Salt and pepper to taste		Juice of 2 lemons	
1	purple onion, cut into quarters and thinly sliced	1/2	cup olive oil

Cut the kernels from the ears of corn with a sharp knife into a large bowl. Boil the potatoes in water to cover in a saucepan until tender. Drain and let stand until cool. Cut into quarters. Cut the tomatoes into halves or quarters. Sprinkle with salt and pepper. Add the potatoes, tomatoes, onion and basil to the corn and mix well. Stir in the crab meat. Whisk the lemon juice and olive oil in a bowl. Pour over the salad and toss lightly to coat. Season with salt and pepper.

Serves 6

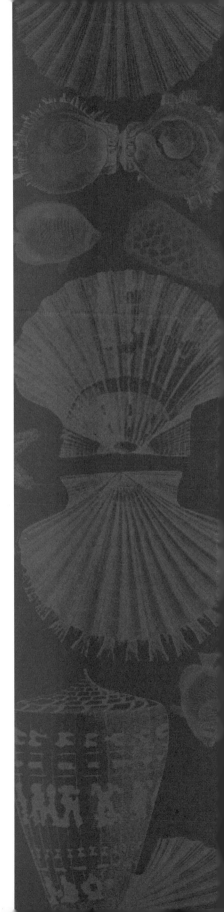

OLD BALDY PASTA SALAD

2	pounds spiral pasta, cooked and drained	1/2	cup green olives and/or black olives
3/4	cup finely chopped bell peppers		Salt and pepper to taste
1/2	cup finely chopped broccoli	1	tablespoons flaked garlic
1	avocado, cut into chunks	1	tablespoon Old Bay seasoning
1	cup cubed cheese		Thyme to taste
1	rib celery, finely chopped	3/4	cup olive oil
1/2	cup cherry tomatoes, whole or halved	3/4	cup balsamic vinegar

Divide the pasta between two bowls with lids. Add one-half of the bell peppers, broccoli, avocado, cheese, celery, tomatoes, olives, salt, pepper, garlic, Old Bay seasoning, thyme, olive oil and vinegar to each bowl of pasta. Cover the bowls and shake to coat. Combine both pasta mixtures in a large serving bowl. Chill, covered, until serving time.

Serves 4 to 6

BROCCOLI SALAD

2	to 3 bunches broccoli	8	ounces bacon, cooked and crumbled
1	tablespoon chopped red onion	1	cup mayonnaise
1/2	cup dried cranberries	1/2	cup sugar
1/2	cup raisins	2	tablespoons white vinegar
1/2	cup sunflower seeds		

Cut the broccoli into bite-size pieces. Combine the broccoli, onion, dried cranberries, raisins, sunflower seeds and bacon in a large bowl and toss to mix. Chill until serving time. Combine the mayonnaise, sugar and vinegar in a small glass bowl and mix well. Pour over the broccoli mixture just before serving and toss to coat.

Serves 8 to 10

BLUEBERRY COBBLER

1	cup sugar
1/2	cup (1 stick) butter, softened
1 1/2	cups all-purpose flour
1	teaspoon cinnamon
3/4	cup half-and-half
3/4	cup sugar
5	teaspoons cinnamon
1/2	cup (1 stick) butter, melted
4	cups blueberries

Beat 1 cup sugar and 1/2 cup softened butter in a mixing bowl until creamy. Add the flour, 1 teaspoon cinnamon and the half-and-half and mix well. Mix 3/4 cup sugar, 5 teaspoons cinnamon and 1/2 cup melted butter in a bowl. Stir in the blueberries. Spoon one-half of the blueberry mixture into a greased baking dish. Drop mounds of the flour mixture over the blueberry mixture. Spoon the remaining blueberry mixture over the top. Bake in a preheated 400-degree oven for 35 to 40 minutes or until cooked through. Serve warm with vanilla ice cream.

Serves 4

PEACH CRISP

6	peaches
1	cup sugar
1	cup self-rising flour
1	egg
1/2	cup (1 stick) butter, melted

Peel the peaches. Cut the peaches into small pieces and place in an 8x8-inch baking pan. Mix the sugar, flour and egg in a bowl. Spoon over the peaches. Pour the butter over the top. Bake in a preheated 325-degree oven for 30 minutes or until golden brown.

Serves 6 to 8

Summer Suppers

Summertime and the livin' is easy. It is a season for indulging in quality time with family and friends without typical routines and hustling. Stretches of longer, warmer days spent in the sunshine and refreshing cool waters stir up everyone's appetite. Under the amber sunset hues of evening, a tasty summer supper will leave your clan with satisfied smiles before settling in to listen to summer tunes or watch the latest blockbuster.

Beginning the day downtown, it is a delight to breeze through the bustling farmers' market on the Cape Fear River, checking off grocery list items with fresh local finds. As you stroll along the city's riverwalk, taking in the sights and sounds, you may find the perfect bouquet to dress up your beach buffet table, and you can discover delectables such as a local catch of grouper, which can be fried with country ham and corn and served with a pepper jelly sauce. Fresh fixin's for a gazpacho and a crisp summer salad, drizzled with light raspberry vinaigrette, are in abundance from local gardens. That evening, chilled pies can be the crowning crowd pleaser—whether the Lemonade, Plantation or Strawberry Pie, everyone will clamor for "just one more piece." A charming summer supper is the perfect way to end the day—so simple.

Ali & Carlos are Engaged!

PLEASE JOIN US
FOR A
SUMMER SUPPER
CELEBRATION

SATURDAY, AUGUST EIGHTEENTH
SEVEN O'CLOCK

474 OCEAN POINT PLACE
WILMINGTON

RSVP*
ANN & BILL
799-7405

POOLSIDE ATTIRE

Summer Suppers

Avocado and Corn Salsa   92

Summer Salad with Raspberry Vinaigrette   92

Warm Potato Salad with Arugula and Bacon   93

Tomato and Watermelon Salad   93

Gazpacho   94

Rigatoni with Sausage and Baby Arugula   94

Pan-Roasted Grouper with Country Ham and Corn Sauté
and Pepper Jelly Sauce   95

Jamaican Jerk Pork Tenderloin   96

Summer Squash Casserole   97

Tomato Pie   97

Tangy Green Beans with Pimento   98

Lemonade Pie   98

Plantation Pie   99

Strawberry Pie   99

Avocado and Corn Salsa

4	avocados	Kernels from 2 ears of roasted
1	sweet onion	corn, or 1 cup drained
1	green bell pepper	canned corn
1	red bell pepper	1/2 cup extra-virgin olive oil
1/4	cup black olives	Juice of 1 lime
1/4	cup green olives	Freshly grated black pepper
1/4	cup fresh jalapeño	1/2 cup fresh cilantro,
	chiles, seeded	chopped
2	large tomatoes	

Chop the avocados, onion, bell peppers, olives, jalapeño chiles and tomatoes into bite-size pieces. Combine with the corn in a large bowl and mix well. Whisk the olive oil, lime juice, pepper and cilantro in a small bowl. Pour over the corn mixture and toss to coat. Let stand for 1 hour before serving. Serve with corn chips.

Serves 6 to 8

Summer Salad with Raspberry Vinaigrette

1	package mixed greens	2 tablespoons chopped
1	cup strawberries, sliced	pecans or sliced almonds
1/2	cup grape halves	1/4 cup light extra-virgin
1	cup mandarin oranges	olive oil
1/4	cup shredded carrots	1/4 cup sugar
1/4	cup crumbled feta cheese	2 tablespoons raspberry
2	tablespoons dried	vinegar
	cranberries	1/4 teaspoon celery salt

Combine the mixed greens, strawberries, grapes, mandarin oranges, carrots, cheese, dried cranberries and pecans in a bowl and toss to mix. Combine the olive oil, sugar, vinegar and celery salt in a container with a lid. Seal the container and shake to mix well. Pour over the salad just before serving and toss to coat.

Serves 4 to 6

Warm Potato Salad with Arugula and Bacon

14 ounces tiny new or fingerling potatoes

Salt and pepper to taste

3/4 cup (1 1/2 sticks) unsalted butter

1/2 cup apple cider vinegar

6 tablespoons sugar

8 slices bacon, cooked and crumbled

4 green onions, thinly sliced

4 cups loosely packed arugula

Boil the potatoes in water to cover in a saucepan for 30 minutes or until fork tender. Drain and cool for 10 minutes. Season with salt and pepper. Heat the butter in a saucepan until it browns and begins to smell nutty. Remove from the heat and strain into a bowl. Mix the vinegar and sugar in a microwave-safe dish. Microwave on High for 1 minute or until the sugar dissolves. Add to the butter and mix well. Season with salt. Keep warm. Combine the potatoes, bacon, green onions and arugula in a bowl and toss to mix. Add the dressing and toss to coat. Serve immediately.

Serves 6 to 8

Tomato and Watermelon Salad

6 cups chopped seedless watermelon

2 pounds summer tomatoes, coarsely chopped

4 teaspoons sugar

1 teaspoon salt

1/2 teaspoon cracked pepper

1 cup thinly sliced quartered red onion

3/4 cup red wine vinegar

1/2 cup extra-virgin olive oil

Combine the watermelon and tomatoes in a large bowl. Add the sugar, salt and pepper and toss to coat. Let stand for several minutes. Add the onion and toss to mix. Whisk the vinegar and olive oil in a bowl. Add to the salad and toss to coat. Chill, covered, for 2 hours. Serve as a side dish or over lettuce.

Serves 4 to 6

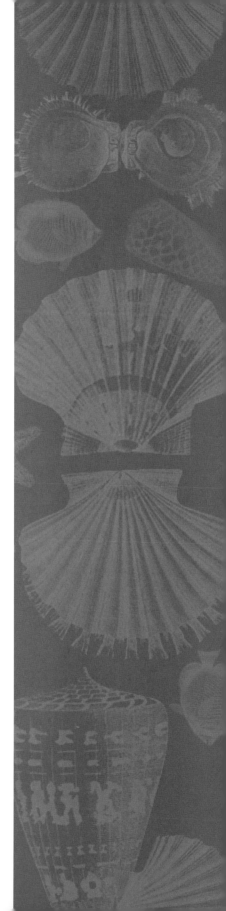

GAZPACHO

6	tomatoes, peeled and chopped
1	purple onion, finely chopped
1	white onion, finely chopped
1	cucumber, peeled, seeded and chopped
1	green bell pepper, finely chopped
1	garlic clove, minced
1/4	cup red wine vinegar
1/4	cup olive oil
4	slices white bread, cut into small pieces

Salt and freshly ground pepper to taste

Process the tomatoes, onions, cucumber, bell pepper, garlic, vinegar, olive oil, bread, salt and pepper in a blender to the desired consistency. Spoon into a nonmetal nonreactive storage container and cover tightly. Chill for 8 to 10 hours or until the flavors meld.

Serves 8

RIGATONI WITH SAUSAGE AND BABY ARUGULA

1	pound rigatoni

Salt to taste

1	pound spicy Italian sausage, casings removed
1	cup chopped sweet onions
1	(14-ounce) can chicken broth
3	cups baby arugula, coarsely chopped
2/3	cup shaved Parmesan cheese

Pepper to taste

Cook the pasta in boiling salted water in a saucepan until al dente. Brown the sausage in a large nonstick skillet over medium heat, stirring until crumbly. Add the onions. Cook for 10 to 12 minutes or until the sausage is cooked through and the onions are soft and translucent. Add the broth. Cook for 3 to 5 minutes or until heated through. Drain the pasta and return to the saucepan. Add the sausage mixture, arugula and cheese and toss to mix well. Season with salt and pepper.

Serves 6

Pan-Roasted Grouper with Country Ham and Corn Sauté and Pepper Jelly Sauce

Pepper Jelly Sauce

2   cups pepper jelly

Juice from 1 lemon

2   tablespoons water

Country Ham and Corn Sauté

8   ounces country ham, thinly sliced

6   cups fresh corn kernels

1/4   cup thinly sliced green onions

Cracked pepper to taste

Pan-Roasted Grouper

6   tablespoons olive oil

8   (6-ounce) pieces grouper, patted dry

Salt and pepper to taste

To prepare the sauce, combine the jelly, lemon juice and water in a container and mix well. Store, covered, in the refrigerator for up to 1 month.

To prepare the sauté, render the ham in a sauté pan over medium heat. Cook for 8 minutes, stirring occasionally. Remove the ham to paper towels to drain, reserving the drippings in the sauté pan. Sauté the corn in the reserved drippings for 6 minutes or just until the corn begins to soften. The corn should be a little crunchy. Return the ham to the sauté pan. Stir in the green onions and pepper.

To prepare the fish, heat the olive oil in an ovenproof skillet over medium-high heat. Sprinkle the fish with salt and pepper and pat dry again. Sear in the hot olive oil for 4 minutes. Place the skillet in a preheated 300-degree oven. Roast for 5 minutes. Remove from the oven. Serve seared side up with the country ham and corn sauté and the pepper jelly sauce.

Serves 8

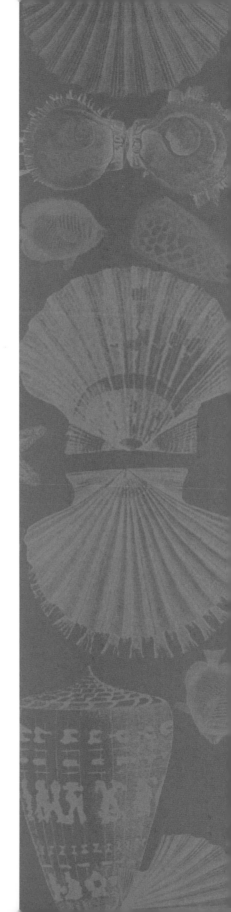

Jamaican Jerk Pork Tenderloin

2	cups chopped green onions
1/2	cup chopped onion
2	tablespoons white vinegar
1	tablespoon soy sauce
1	tablespoon vegetable oil
2	teaspoons kosher salt
2	teaspoons chopped fresh thyme
2	teaspoons brown sugar
2	teaspoons chopped peeled ginger
1	teaspoon ground allspice
1/4	teaspoon nutmeg
1/4	teaspoon pepper
1/8	teaspoon cinnamon
2	garlic cloves, minced
2	habanero chiles, seeded and chopped
1	(1 1/2-pound) pork tenderloin, trimmed

Pulse the green onions, onion, vinegar, soy sauce, oil, kosher salt, thyme, brown sugar, ginger, allspice, nutmeg, pepper, cinnamon, garlic and chiles in a blender or food processor until smooth. The mixture will be thick.

Cut the pork lengthwise to but not through the other side. Open the pork, laying each side flat. Cut each half lengthwise to but not through the other side. Place in a large sealable plastic bag. Add the marinade and seal the bag. Marinate in the refrigerator for 3 to 24 hours.

Drain the pork, discarding the marinade. Place the pork on a grill rack coated with nonstick cooking spray. Grill over medium heat to 160 degrees on a meat thermometer. The inside should be slightly pink.

Note: Be sure to wear plastic gloves to protect your hands when handling habanero chiles.

Serves 4

SUMMER SQUASH CASSEROLE

3	pounds yellow squash, chopped	1	tablespoon sugar
Salt to taste		1	teaspoon salt
1/2	cup chopped onion	1/2	teaspoon pepper
2	eggs	1/4	cup (1/2 stick) butter, melted
1/4	cup (1/2 stick) butter	1/2	cup bread crumbs

Cook the squash in boiling salted water in a saucepan for 20 minutes or until tender; drain. Mash the squash. Add the onion, eggs, 1/4 cup butter, the sugar, 1 teaspoon salt and the pepper and mix well. Spoon into a deep baking dish. Pour the melted butter over the squash. Sprinkle the bread crumbs over the top. Bake in a preheated 375-degree oven for 1 hour or until brown.

Serves 12

TOMATO PIE

1	unbaked (9-inch) pie shell	1	cup basil leaves, chopped
4	tomatoes	2	cups (8 ounces) shredded mozzarella cheese
Salt and pepper to taste		1/2	cup (2 ounces) grated Parmesan cheese
1/2	cup light mayonnaise		
1 1/2	teaspoons minced garlic		

Bake the pie shell in a preheated 375-degree oven until brown. Remove from the oven and maintain the oven temperature. Cut the tomatoes into slices and drain on paper towels. Sprinkle the tomatoes with salt and pepper. Combine the mayonnaise, garlic, basil and 1/2 cup of the mozzarella cheese in a bowl and mix well. Cover the bottom of the hot pie shell with one-half of the remaining mozzarella cheese. Layer the tomatoes and mayonnaise mixture one-half at a time over the cheese layer, ending with the mayonnaise mixture. Sprinkle with the remaining mozzarella cheese and the Parmesan cheese. Bake for 30 to 40 minutes or until heated through.

Serves 4 to 6

TANGY GREEN BEANS WITH PIMENTO

1 1/2	pounds green beans, trimmed	1/4	cup red wine vinegar
3	slices bacon	1	teaspoon sugar
1	onion, chopped	1/2	teaspoon salt
3	garlic cloves, minced	1/2	teaspoon pepper
1	(2-ounce) jar chopped pimento, drained	1/2	teaspoon crushed cumin seeds

Cook the green beans in boiling water to cover in a saucepan for 4 to 5 minutes or until tender-crisp. Drain the green beans and plunge immediately into ice water to stop the cooking process. Drain and set aside. Cook the bacon in a large skillet until crisp. Remove to paper towels to drain. Drain the skillet, reserving 2 tablespoons of the bacon drippings. Sauté the onion and garlic in the reserved drippings over medium-high heat until tender. Stir in the pimento, vinegar, sugar, salt, pepper and cumin seeds. Stir in the green beans. Reduce the heat and simmer for 5 minutes. Crumble the bacon over the top and serve warm.

Serves 6

LEMONADE PIE

1	(3-ounce) package lemon instant pudding mix	1	(6-ounce) can frozen lemonade concentrate, partially thawed
1	(3-ounce) package vanilla instant pudding mix		Juice of 1 lemon
1	(10-ounce) can evaporated milk	1	(9-inch) graham cracker pie shell
16	ounces light cream cheese, softened		Whipped topping for garnish
		8	pieces sliced lemon rind for garnish

Whisk the pudding mixes and evaporated milk in a bowl until thickened. Beat the cream cheese at medium speed in a mixing bowl until fluffy. Add the lemonade concentrate and lemon juice and beat until blended. Add the pudding mixture and mix well. Pour into the pie shell. Freeze until firm. Garnish with whipped topping and lemon rind.

Serves 8

PLANTATION PIE

1 (14-ounce) can sweetened condensed milk
1/4 cup lemon juice
1 (16-ounce) can crushed pineapple
1 cup shredded coconut
1 cup walnuts, chopped
16 ounces whipped topping
2 (9-inch) graham cracker pie shells

Mix the condensed milk and lemon juice in a large bowl. Add the pineapple, coconut and walnuts and mix well. Fold in the whipped topping. Spoon into the pie shells. Chill for 2 hours before serving.

Serves 16

STRAWBERRY PIE

1 1/2 cups sugar
Dash of salt
1/4 cup cornstarch
1 1/2 cups hot water
6 tablespoons strawberry gelatin powder
4 cups strawberries, sliced
8 ounces cream cheese, softened
2 baked (9-inch) pie shells

Mix the sugar, salt and cornstarch in a saucepan. Add the hot water. Bring to a boil. Cook until the mixture turns clear. Add the gelatin and stir until dissolved. Add the strawberries. Spread one-half of the cream cheese into each pie shell. Top with the strawberry mixture. Chill for 2 hours before serving.

Serves 12 to 16

Carolina Traditions

As the summer winds down, when the mornings begin to cool and the sun sets a little earlier, it is certain that beach season has come to a close. Now it is time to get ready for back-to-school activities. Always the optimists, North Carolinians show their enthusiasm for their university and college teams, adorning the colors of favorite alma maters. With so many strong athletic programs in the state, intense but congenial rivalries are common among true, loyal sports fans!

Wilmington also has claim to many celebrated sports stars. From the sidelines, locals have watched athletes become national heroes representing all sports, including Tennis Hall of Fame star Althea Gibson; Olympic Gold Medalist boxer Sugar Ray Leonard; baseball World Series Champion Trot Nixon; Pro Football Hall of Famers Sonny Jurgensen and Roman Gabriel; and celebrated basketball superstars Meadowlark Lemon and Michael Jordan. We are proud fans!

North Carolina seems to have invented tailgating, too! Well maybe not . . . but don't tell that to the locals. Good food and team competition are taken very seriously. It's best to enjoy yourself and please the rowdy crowds with game day favorites. If you serve fans savory Sausage Bites, Buffalo Chicken Dip, Pizza Bread, and Tarheel Tea, soon you, too, will have your own loyal following.

Carolina Traditions

Tarheel Tea   104

Hot Cheese Squares   104

Sausage Bites   105

Italian Layer Dip   105

Buffalo Chicken Dip   106

Seahawk Salsa   106

Spiced Steamed Shrimp   107

Simple Cocktail Sauce   107

Stuffed Potatoes   108

Black Bean Chili   109

Beef or Chicken Kabobs   110

Pizza Bread   110

Crazy-Good Peanut Butter Pie   111

Game Day Cookies   111

TARHEEL TEA

1	ounce bourbon
3	dashes of bitters
4	ounces ginger ale
1	slice orange
1	cherry

Pour the bourbon over crushed ice in a cocktail glass. Add the bitters and ginger ale. Squeeze the orange slice into the mixture. Add the cherry.

Serves 1

HOT CHEESE SQUARES

16	ounces Pepper Jack cheese, shredded
16	ounces sharp Cheddar cheese, shredded
1	(5-ounce) can evaporated milk
1	tablespoon all-purpose flour
1	teaspoon salt
1	teaspoon pepper
4	eggs, beaten
1	(4-ounce) can green chiles

Mix the Pepper Jack cheese and Cheddar cheese in a bowl. Spread in a 9×13-inch baking dish. Combine the evaporated milk, flour, salt and pepper in a bowl and mix until smooth. Add the eggs and mix well. Stir in the green chiles. Pour over the cheese. Bake in a preheated 350-degree oven for 45 minutes or until brown. Cool on a wire rack. Cut into squares.

Serves 20 to 24

SAUSAGE BITES

1   pound hot bulk pork sausage
1 1/2   cups (6 ounces) shredded sharp Cheddar cheese,
       at room temperature
1 1/2   cups baking mix

Combine the sausage, cheese and baking mix in a large bowl and mix well. Shape into small balls and place on a baking sheet. Bake in a preheated 350-degree oven for 15 minutes. Cool on a wire rack.

Serves about 24

ITALIAN LAYER DIP

8   ounces cream cheese, softened
1/2   cup sour cream
1   teaspoon oregano
1/8   teaspoon garlic powder
1/8   teaspoon crushed red pepper
1/2   cup pizza sauce
1/4   cup chopped green bell pepper
1/4   cup chopped onion
1/2   cup chopped pepperoni
1/2   cup (2 ounces) shredded mozzarella cheese

Beat the cream cheese, sour cream, oregano, garlic powder and red pepper in a bowl until smooth. Spread evenly in an 8×8-inch baking dish. Spread the pizza sauce over the cream cheese layer. Sprinkle with the bell pepper, onion and pepperoni. Bake in a preheated 350-degree oven for 10 minutes. Sprinkle with the mozzarella cheese. Bake for 5 minutes or until the mozzarella cheese melts.

Serves 8 to 10

Buffalo Chicken Dip

1½ pounds chicken breasts, boiled and chopped
16 ounces cream cheese, softened
1   cup blue cheese salad dressing
3/4 cup hot pepper sauce
8   ounces sharp Cheddar cheese, shredded

Combine the chicken, cream cheese, salad dressing and hot sauce in a bowl and mix well. Spoon into a 9×13-inch baking dish. Sprinkle with the Cheddar cheese. Bake in a preheated 350-degree oven for 30 minutes. Serve with tortilla chips.

Serves 6 to 10

Seahawk Salsa

1   (15-ounce) can black beans, drained and rinsed
1   (10-ounce) package frozen corn, thawed
2   tomatoes, chopped
1/2 red bell pepper, chopped
1/3 cup chopped fresh cilantro
1/4 red onion, chopped
3   tablespoons fresh lime juice
1   jalapeño chile, seeded and chopped (optional)
Pepper to taste

Combine the beans, corn, tomatoes, bell pepper, cilantro, onion, lime juice, jalapeño chile and pepper in a bowl and mix well. Chill until serving time. Serve with blue corn chips.

Serves 10 to 15

SPICED STEAMED SHRIMP

6   (12-ounce) cans beer
1/2   cup white vinegar
1   tablespoon kosher salt
1   small lemon, cut into halves
10   pounds fresh shrimp (12 pounds with heads on)
1   cup Old Bay seasoning

Pour the beer and vinegar into a large stockpot. Add the kosher salt and lemon halves. Bring to a rolling boil. Place a steamer rack in the stockpot. Cover the rack with a layer of the shrimp and sprinkle with Old Bay seasoning. Repeat the layers until all the shrimp and seasoning is used. Steam, tightly covered, for 10 minutes or until the shrimp turn pink. Remove the shrimp to cool.

Serves 8 to 10

SIMPLE COCKTAIL SAUCE

1   cup ketchup
1   tablespoon grated horseradish
4   dashes of Worcestershire sauce
1   tablespoon fresh lemon juice

Combine the ketchup, horseradish, Worcestershire sauce and lemon juice in a bowl and mix well. Chill until serving time. Adjust the heat by adding more or less horseradish. Another option is to serve extra horseradish on the side.

Makes 1 cup

STUFFED POTATOES

4 large baking potatoes

1/4 cup (1/2 stick) butter

1/2 cup chopped green onions

1/2 cup chopped green bell pepper

1/2 cup chopped red bell pepper

3 ounces cream cheese, softened

1 cup mayonnaise

1 cup sour cream

1 cup chopped ham (optional)

1 cup (4 ounces) shredded Cheddar cheese

Salt and pepper to taste

Chopped fresh chives for garnish

Place the potatoes on a foil-lined baking sheet. Bake in a preheated 395-degree oven for 30 to 45 minutes or until tender. Reduce the oven temperature to 375 degrees. Let stand until cool enough to handle. Melt the butter in a small skillet over medium heat. Add the green onions and bell peppers. Cook for 5 minutes or until tender. Cut the cooled potatoes into halves lengthwise.

Scoop out the potato into a mixing bowl, leaving a 1/4-inch-thick shell. Set the potato shells aside. Add the pepper mixture, cream cheese, mayonnaise, sour cream, ham, Cheddar cheese, salt and pepper to the potatoes and mix well. Spoon into the reserved potato shells and place on a baking sheet. Bake for 30 minutes or until the cheese melts. Garnish with chives.

Serves 8

BLACK BEAN CHILI

1	pound boneless top sirloin steak, cut into 1-inch pieces
2	onions, chopped
1	green bell pepper, chopped
1	jalapeño chile, seeded and chopped
3	garlic cloves, minced
1 1/2	teaspoons salt
3	tablespoons olive oil
1	(28-ounce) can crushed tomatoes
1	(12-ounce) bottle dark beer
2	tablespoons chili powder
1	tablespoon ground cumin
1	teaspoon sugar
2	teaspoons oregano
1 1/2	teaspoons black pepper
1/4	teaspoon red pepper
2	cups beef broth
3	(15-ounce) cans black beans, drained and rinsed

Shredded Cheddar cheese for garnish

Cook the beef, onions, bell pepper, jalapeño chile, garlic and 1/2 teaspoon
of the salt in the olive oil in a large Dutch oven over medium-high heat for
8 minutes or until the beef browns and the vegetables are tender, stirring constantly.
Stir in the remaining 1 teaspoon salt, the tomatoes, 1/2 cup of the beer, the chili
powder, cumin, sugar, oregano, black pepper and red pepper. Simmer for 30 minutes,
stirring occasionally. Stir in the remaining beer, the broth and beans. Simmer
for 45 minutes or until heated through, stirring occasionally. Ladle into soup bowls
and garnish with cheese.

Serves 12

Beef or Chicken Kabobs

2 to 3 pounds beef pieces or chicken pieces

1/2 cup soy sauce

1/2 cup Worcestershire sauce

1/4 cup olive oil

3 garlic cloves, crushed

Juice of 2 lemons

Place the beef in a sealable plastic bag. Whisk the soy sauce, Worcestershire sauce, olive oil, garlic and lemon juice in a bowl. Pour over the beef and seal the bag. Marinate in the refrigerator for 2 to 24 hours. Soak wooden skewers in water for 30 minutes. Thread the beef onto the skewers and place on a grill rack. Grill over medium heat until cooked through.

Serves 4 to 6

Pizza Bread

3 loaves frozen white bread dough, thawed

1 1/4 pounds yellow American cheese, sliced and cut into halves

1 (8-ounce) package sliced pepperoni

Italian seasoning to taste

Stretch out one loaf of the dough on a work surface; cut through the middle to butterfly. Layer one-sixth of the cheese, one-third of the pepperoni and one-sixth of the cheese over the dough. Sprinkle with Italian seasoning. Pull the sides of the bread dough over the layers and pinch the dough together at the top to enclose. Sprinkle with Italian seasoning. Wrap in foil sprayed with nonstick cooking spray. Repeat the procedure with the remaining bread dough, cheese, pepperoni and Italian seasoning. Bake in a preheated 350-degree oven for 40 to 50 minutes or until the loaves are golden brown. Remove from the oven and let stand for 10 minutes to cool. Cut into slices.

Makes 3 loaves

CRAZY-GOOD PEANUT BUTTER PIE

4	ounces cream cheese, softened	1	(5-ounce) package chocolate instant pudding mix
1	cup creamy peanut butter	2	cups milk
1	tablespoon sugar	Candy-coated peanut butter	
1	tablespoon milk		candies for garnish
12	ounces whipped topping		
1	(9-inch) chocolate graham cracker pie shell		

Combine the cream cheese, peanut butter, sugar and 1 tablespoon milk in a bowl and beat until blended and smooth. Stir in 1 1/2 cups of the whipped topping. Spread over the bottom of the pie shell. Combine the pudding mix and 2 cups milk in a bowl and stir until thickened. Add 1 cup of the remaining whipped topping and stir gently until combined. Spread over the peanut butter mixture. Spread the remaining whipped topping evenly over the pudding layer. Garnish with candies. Chill in the refrigerator for 8 to 10 hours before serving.

Serves 8

GAME DAY COOKIES

1 1/3	cups rolled oats	1/2	cup (1 stick) butter, melted
1/2	cup packed brown sugar	1	egg
1/2	cup granulated sugar	1	teaspoon vanilla extract
1 1/3	cups all-purpose flour	1/2	cup pecans, chopped
1	teaspoon baking powder	1	cup (6 ounces) semisweet chocolate chips
1	teaspoon baking soda		
1/4	teaspoon salt		

Mix the oats, brown sugar, granulated sugar, flour, baking powder, baking soda and salt in a large bowl. Beat the butter, egg and vanilla in a large mixing bowl. Add the oat mixture and mix well. Stir in the pecans and chocolate chips. Shape into walnut-size balls. Place 2 inches apart on a cookie sheet. Bake in a preheated 350-degree oven for 11 to 13 minutes or until golden brown. Cool on a wire rack.

Makes 2 dozen

Pig Pickin'

Barbecue lovers are embroiled in more than just criticism over which state has perfected the ultimate recipe. Individual states also vary geographically in their variations on ingredients, methods, and cuts of meat. North Carolina is no exception. Given the coastal location of Wilmington, we offer here tips for "Eastern Style" North Carolina barbecue. In recent years the subtleties between this and "Western Style" have diminished, but purists still demand Eastern Style as follows:

— Cooks use the entire pig, as opposed to just the shoulders or other portions, split in two from the stomach to the spine and cleaned of internal organs.

— Only dry spices are added, with a little vinegar to keep the meat moist; preparers do not use heavy marinades or sauces during cooking.

— After the pig is cooked, all the meat, skin, and fat is finely chopped together; optional hot sauces can be added by the eater.

— Common sides served with Eastern Style North Carolina barbecue include hush puppies, which are basically made from cornmeal and onions mixed with a binding agent and deep fried in round or oblong nuggets; mayonnaise-based cole slaw (Western favors a vinegar-based style slaw); and ALWAYS sweetened iced tea.

Jackson's Big Oak Barbecue in Wilmington has served up outstanding plates of barbecue for more than twenty-five years. They believe the reason for its ongoing popularity lies in one ingredient: the light, vinegar-based sauce.

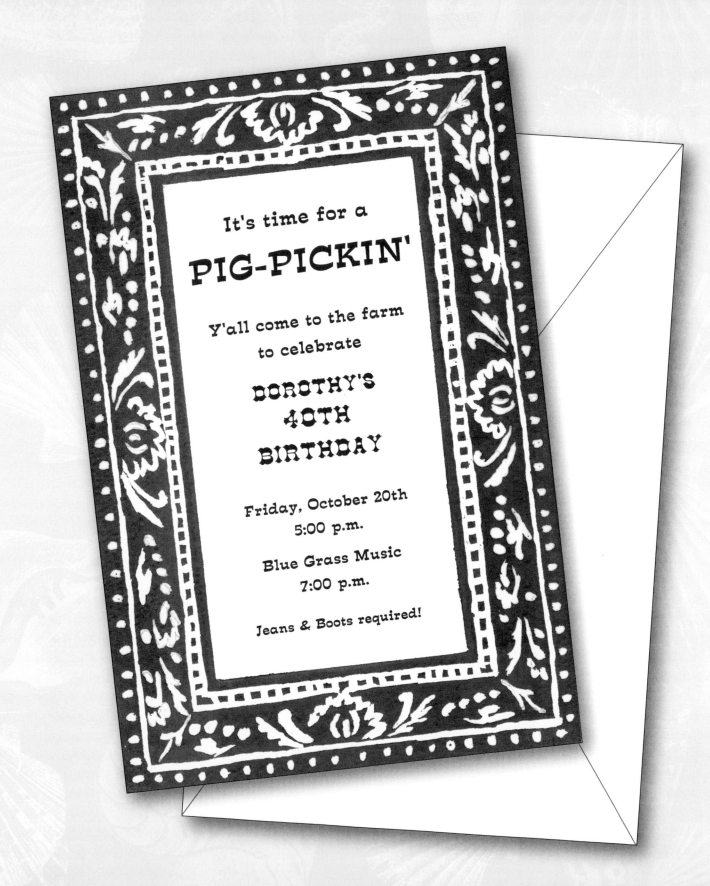

It's time for a

PIG-PICKIN'

Y'all come to the farm
to celebrate

DOROTHY'S
40TH
BIRTHDAY

Friday, October 20th
5:00 p.m.

Blue Grass Music
7:00 p.m.

Jeans & Boots required!

Pig Pickin'

Southern Sweet Tea   116

Best-Ever Cheese Ring   116

Traditional Pulled Pork   117

Eastern Carolina Barbecue Sauce   117

Loaded Barbecue Potato Casserole   118

Fallin'-Off-the-Bone Ribs   119

Tropical Edamame Salad   119

Barbecue Slaw   120

Corn Relish Salad   120

Three-Bean Baked Beans   121

Fresh Collard Greens   121

Pumpkin Biscuits with Maple Ham   122

Banana Pudding   122

Favorite Chocolate Cake   123

SOUTHERN SWEET TEA

8   cups water
12   small tea bags
1 1/2   cups sugar
1   (12-ounce) can frozen lemonade concentrate
Mint leaves for garnish

Bring the water and tea bags to a boil in a saucepan over high heat. Let steep for 5 minutes. Remove the tea bags. Add the sugar and lemonade concentrate and mix well. Pour into a 1-gallon container. Fill with cold water. Serve over ice garnished with mint.

Makes 1 gallon

BEST-EVER CHEESE RING

16   ounces sharp Cheddar cheese, shredded
1   cup chopped toasted pecans
3/4   cup mayonnaise
1   onion, grated
1   garlic clove, minced
1/2   teaspoon Tabasco sauce
1   cup strawberry preserves

Line a ring mold with plastic wrap, leaving enough overhang to cover the top. Combine the cheese, pecans, mayonnaise, onion, garlic and Tabasco sauce in a bowl and mix well. Pack into the prepared mold and cover with the plastic wrap. Chill for several hours or until serving time. To serve, uncover and invert onto a serving platter. Spoon the preserves into the center. Serve with crackers.

Serves 15

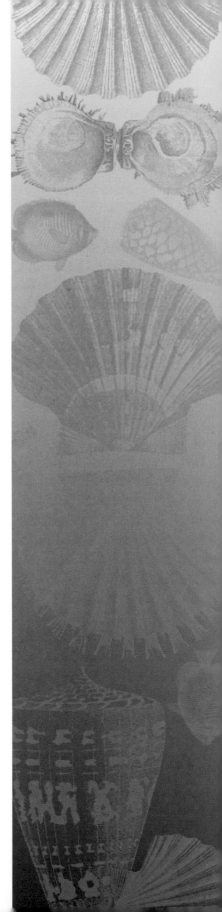

TRADITIONAL PULLED PORK

2	teaspoons cayenne pepper
1	tablespoon onion powder
2	tablespoons garlic powder
2	tablespoons black pepper
2	tablespoons salt
2	tablespoons paprika
1	(6- to 8-pound) pork shoulder roast or Boston butt roast
2	cups water
1 1/2	cups apple cider vinegar
3	tablespoons Worcestershire sauce

Mix the cayenne pepper, onion powder, garlic powder, black pepper, salt and paprika in a bowl to make a dry rub. Place the pork in a 9×13-inch dish. Press the rub on all sides of the pork. Chill, covered, for 4 to 10 hours. Mix the water, vinegar and Worcestershire sauce in a large roasting pan with a lid. Place the pork in the mixture. Bake, covered, in a preheated 300-degree oven for 5 to 6 hours or until cooked through. Let stand until cool enough to handle. Shred the pork with a fork, discarding the fat, skin and bones. Serve with barbecue sauce and coleslaw.

Serves 10 to 12

EASTERN CAROLINA BARBECUE SAUCE

1	gallon (16 cups) vinegar
1	cup sugar
1	cup salt
1	(18- or 20-ounce) bottle barbecue sauce
1	(12- or 18-ounce) bottle ketchup
1/2	to 1 (1-ounce) box red pepper
1/2	to 1 (1-ounce) box black pepper

Combine the vinegar, sugar, salt, barbecue sauce, ketchup, red pepper and black pepper in a bowl and mix well. Serve with smoked pork.

Makes about 5 quarts

LOADED BARBECUE POTATO CASSEROLE

2 1/2 pounds Yukon Gold potatoes, peeled and chopped
6   to 8 slices bacon
2   cups milk
1   cup (4 ounces) shredded Pepper Jack cheese
4   ounces cream cheese, cut into cubes
2   cups (8 ounces) shredded sharp Cheddar cheese
Salt and pepper to taste
1   cup light sour cream
1   (4-ounce) can chopped green chiles, drained
1   cup (4 ounces) shredded sharp Cheddar cheese
2 1/2 cups shredded barbecued pork or beef
3/4   cup barbecue sauce

Boil the potatoes in water to cover in a saucepan until tender. Cook the bacon in a skillet over medium-high heat until crisp. Remove to paper towels to drain. Crumble the bacon and set aside. Drain the potatoes and return to the saucepan. Add the milk, Pepper Jack cheese, cream cheese, 2 cups Cheddar cheese, the salt and pepper and mash well. Stir in the sour cream, green chiles and crumbled bacon.

Spoon into a lightly greased 9×13-inch baking dish. Sprinkle with 1 cup Cheddar cheese. Spread the pork evenly over the cheese. Drizzle the barbecue sauce over the pork. Bake in a preheated 350-degree oven for 35 to 45 minutes or until heated through.

Serves 8 to 10

FALLIN'-OFF-THE-BONE RIBS

6	short pork spareribs	1	teaspoon sage
2	cups beer	1	tablespoon salt substitute
1	cup honey	3	tablespoons lemon juice
1	teaspoon dry mustard	1	tablespoon Worcestershire
1	tablespoon chili powder		sauce

Boil the spareribs in water to cover in a saucepan for 15 to 20 minutes. Remove from the heat to cool. Place the ribs in a large bowl. Mix the beer, honey, dry mustard, chili powder, sage, salt substitute, lemon juice and Worcestershire sauce in a bowl. Pour over the ribs. Marinate, covered, in the refrigerator for 12 hours or longer, turning several times. Drain the ribs, reserving the marinade. Place the ribs on a grill rack. Grill 4 inches from the heat source until dark brown and glazed, turning frequently and brushing with the reserved marinade.

Serves 6

TROPICAL EDAMAME SALAD

2	cups shelled edamame	2	tablespoons fresh cilantro
1 1/2	cups whole kernel corn	1	tablespoon extra-virgin
1 1/2	cups chopped mangoes		olive oil
1	cup chopped tomato	1	tablespoon fresh
1/2	cup chopped red		lime juice
	bell pepper		Dash of salt
1/3	cup chopped red onion	1/4	teaspoon pepper

Prepare the edamame using the package directions. Drain and rinse in cold water. Combine the edamame, corn, mangoes, tomato, bell pepper, onion, cilantro, olive oil, lime juice, salt and pepper in a bowl and toss to mix.

Serves 8

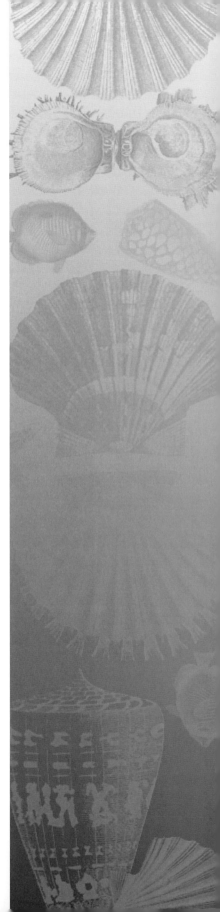

BARBECUE SLAW

1	green cabbage, shredded
1/2	purple cabbage, shredded
2	carrots, shredded
2	onions, thinly sliced
1	cup sugar
1	cup vinegar
3/4	cup vegetable oil
1	teaspoon salt
1	teaspoon dry mustard
1	teaspoon celery seeds

Mix the green cabbage, purple cabbage, carrots, onions and 3/4 cup of the sugar in a bowl. Combine the remaining 1/4 cup sugar, the vinegar, oil, salt, dry mustard and celery seeds in a small saucepan and mix well. Bring to a boil; remove from the heat. Pour over the cabbage mixture and toss to coat. Chill, covered, for 8 to 10 hours before serving.

Serves 12 to 15

CORN RELISH SALAD

2	(16-ounce) cans whole kernel corn, drained
1	(15-ounce) can black beans, drained and rinsed
1	cup chopped bell pepper
1/2	cup chopped onion
1/4	cup vinegar
1	tablespoon sugar
1/2	cup fresh cilantro, or dried cilantro to taste
11/2	teaspoons garlic powder

Salt and pepper to taste

Combine the corn, beans, bell pepper and onion in a bowl and mix well. Mix the vinegar, sugar, cilantro, garlic powder, salt and pepper in a bowl. Pour over the salad and mix well. Chill, covered, until serving time.

Serves 6

THREE-BEAN BAKED BEANS

8	ounces ground beef	1/3	cup packed brown sugar
5	slices bacon	1/4	cup granulated sugar
1/2	cup chopped onion	1/4	cup ketchup
1	(32-ounce) can pork and beans	1/4	cup barbecue sauce
1	(15-ounce) can butter beans, drained and rinsed	2	tablespoons molasses
		2	tablespoons mustard
1	(16-ounce) can kidney beans, drained and rinsed	1/2	teaspoon chili powder
		1/2	teaspoon salt

Brown the ground beef, bacon and onion in a large skillet over medium heat, stirring until the ground beef is crumbly; drain. Add the pork and beans, butter beans and kidney beans and mix well. Mix the brown sugar, granulated sugar, ketchup, barbecue sauce, molasses, mustard, chili powder and salt in a bowl. Stir into the bean mixture. Spoon into an ungreased 2 1/2-quart baking dish. Bake in a preheated 350-degree oven for 1 hour or until thickened.

Serves 12

FRESH COLLARD GREENS

1	gallon (16 cups) water	1	tablespoon seasoned salt
1	(14-ounce) can chicken broth or vegetable broth	1 1/2	teaspoons salt
1/3	pound bacon or ham hocks, cut into 1-inch strips	1/4	teaspoon pepper
		1/4	teaspoon garlic powder
		1	large bunch fresh collard greens
1	tablespoon hot pepper sauce		Butter to taste

Bring the water and broth to a boil in a large stockpot. Add the bacon, hot sauce, seasoned salt, salt, pepper and garlic powder. Reduce the heat to medium or medium-low. Cook for 1 hour. Wash the collard greens well. Remove the middle stems from the leaves. Stack several leaves at a time together and roll up. Cut into 1-inch slices. Add to the bacon mixture. Cook for 1 hour; drain. Add butter and place in a serving bowl.

Serves 6

Pumpkin Biscuits with Maple Ham

4	cups all-purpose flour	1 1/2	cups pumpkin purée
2 1/2	teaspoons baking powder	2	tablespoons honey
2	teaspoons salt	1/2	cup vanilla yogurt
2	teaspoons ginger	2	tablespoons low-fat milk
1/2	teaspoon pepper	24	pieces maple ham
1	cup (2 sticks) unsalted butter		Pumpkin butter

Mix the flour, baking powder, salt, ginger and pepper in a large bowl. Cut in the butter with a pastry blender or with two knives until crumbly. Mix the pumpkin and honey in a bowl. Stir into the floured mixture just until combined. Mix the yogurt and milk in a small bowl. Add to the pumpkin mixture and stir just until the mixture clings together. Roll the dough 3/4 inch thick on a floured surface. Cut with a large pumpkin or maple leaf cookie cutter. Place 1 inch apart on a greased or nonstick baking sheet. Bake in a preheated 400-degree oven for 25 to 30 minutes or until golden brown. Serve with the ham and pumpkin butter.

Serves 24

Banana Pudding

2	(7-ounce) packages butter cookies	8	ounces cream cheese, softened
6	to 8 bananas, sliced	1	(14-ounce) can sweetened condensed milk
2	cups milk		
1	(4-ounce) package French vanilla instant pudding mix	12	ounces whipped topping

Line the bottom of a 9×13-inch dish with one-half of the cookies. Layer the bananas over the cookies. Combine the milk and pudding mix in a mixing bowl and mix well. Beat the cream cheese and condensed milk in a mixing bowl until smooth. Fold in the whipped topping. Stir into the pudding mixture until blended. Pour over the layers. Cover the top with the remaining cookies. Chill, covered, until serving time.

Serves 12

Favorite Chocolate Cake

Cake

1	(2-layer) package butter recipe fudge cake mix
4	eggs
3/4	cup vegetable oil
3/4	cup sugar
1/4	cup milk
1	(4-ounce) package chocolate instant pudding mix
1	cup sour cream
1	teaspoon vanilla extract
1	cup (6 ounces) miniature semisweet chocolate chips
1	(4-ounce) bar German's sweet chocolate, grated

Chocolate Icing

6	tablespoons butter, softened
1	(1-pound) package confectioners' sugar, sifted
3	ounces unsweetened baking chocolate, melted
	Milk

To prepare the cake, combine the cake mix, eggs, oil, sugar, milk, pudding mix, sour cream and vanilla in a mixing bowl. Beat at medium speed for 2 minutes. Fold in the chocolate chips and German's sweet chocolate. Spoon into a greased and floured bundt pan. Bake in a preheated 350-degree oven for 50 to 55 minutes or until the cake tests done. Cool in the pan for 15 minutes. Invert onto a cake plate.

To prepare the icing, cream the butter and one-half of the confectioners' sugar in a mixing bowl. Add the remaining confectioners' sugar and chocolate and mix well. Add enough milk to reach the desired spreading consistency. Spread over the warm cake. Serve warm.

Serves 12

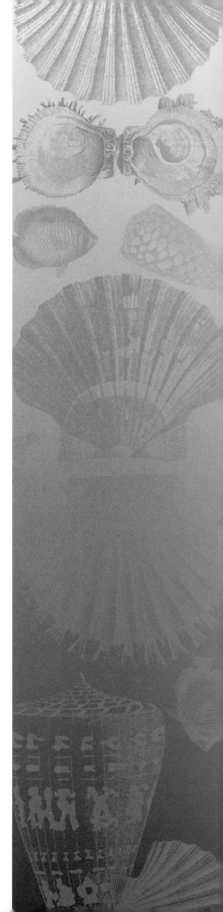

Flotilla Party

The weekend after Thanksgiving welcomes the North Carolina Holiday Flotilla event in Wrightsville Beach. Months of planning go into the event that, for more than twenty-five years, has been considered the kickoff of the holiday season. Anyone with a boat and some imagination for decorating their vessel can register to participate in this Christmas parade on water.

The event was originally marketed as a way to extend the tourist season at the beach. It has developed into a time-honored tradition that brings family and friends together in southeastern North Carolina. Locals and visitors—around 50,000 total—line the parade route from Bradley Creek, to Motts Channel, to Banks Channel, and on to Masonboro Inlet. The flotilla can be viewed by boat, on land, or from a dock. Judges stationed on Banks Channel in front of the Blockade Runner Beach Resort critique the entries and award winners in separate categories along with one Best in Show. The evening's event culminates in a fireworks show that rivals that of Independence Day festivities.

Whether you entertain before, during, or after the event, your guests can look forward to something other than Thanksgiving leftovers. Traditional Southern dishes complement the jubilant atmosphere and need for warmth!

Come enjoy the

FLOTILLA
Boat Parade & Fireworks

from our porch

Saturday, November 26

6:00 p.m.

841 Shore Drive

Wrightsville Beach

Flotilla Party

Flo-tini   128

Crab Bake   128

Chicken Chimichanga Dip   129

Sweet-and-Spicy Walnuts   129

Autumn Squash Soup   130

Pear and Smoked Gouda Salad   131

Turkey Melt Casserole   131

Shrimp and Grits   132

Flotilla Chili   133

Broccoli Corn Bread   134

Corn and Cheese Fritters   134

Rum Cake   135

Mud Pie 135

FLO-TINI

5	ounces vanilla vodka
5	ounces pineapple juice
Juice of 1/2 lime	
1/2	teaspoon confectioners' sugar
2	thin lime wedges for garnish

Pour the vodka, pineapple juice and ice in a martini shaker. Add the lime juice and confectioners' sugar and shake well. Strain into two martini glasses. Garnish each with a thin lime wedge.

Serves 2

CRAB BAKE

6	ounces fresh lump crab meat, shells removed and meat flaked
2	tablespoons chopped onion
8	ounces cream cheese, softened
1/2	teaspoon horseradish
1/4	teaspoon salt
1	tablespoon milk
Grated Parmesan cheese	
Paprika	
Slivered almonds	

Combine the crab meat, onion, cream cheese, horseradish, salt and milk in a bowl and mix well. Spread in a shallow baking dish. Top with Parmesan cheese, paprika and almonds. Bake in a preheated 375-degree oven for 15 minutes. Serve with crackers.

Serves 6 to 8

CHICKEN CHIMICHANGA DIP

1	(12-ounce) can chicken, flaked
8	ounces light cream cheese, softened
1	cup light mayonnaise
2	cups (8 ounces) shredded light Mexican cheese
1	(4-ounce) can chopped green chiles
2	tablespoons chopped jalapeño chiles

Combine the chicken, cream cheese, mayonnaise, Mexican cheese, green chiles and jalapeño chiles in a bowl and mix well. Spoon into a baking dish. Bake in a preheated 350-degree oven for 25 minutes. Serve with tortilla chips.

Makes about 4 cups

SWEET-AND-SPICY WALNUTS

1	egg white
1	tablespoon water
1/2	cup sugar
1/2	teaspoon allspice
1/2	teaspoon cinnamon
1/2	teaspoon salt
1 1/2	cups walnut halves

Beat the egg white with the water at high speed in a mixing bowl until foamy but not stiff. Mix the sugar, allspice, cinnamon and salt in a bowl. Place one-half of the walnuts in a bowl. Add a spoonful of the beaten egg white and stir to coat. Place the coated walnuts in a strainer over a bowl. Spoon one-half of the sugar mixture over the walnuts and toss to coat.

Spread in a single layer on a greased baking sheet. Repeat the process with the remaining walnuts and sugar mixture. Bake in a preheated 300-degree oven for 30 minutes, stirring every 10 minutes. Cool on the baking sheet, stirring occasionally to prevent sticking.

Serves 12

Autumn Squash Soup

3	slices bacon
1	cup chopped onion
2/3	cup chopped celery
3	garlic cloves, minced
4	cups chopped peeled butternut squash
1	cup chopped carrots
4	cups fat-free less-sodium chicken broth
1/2	teaspoon ground cumin
1/8	teaspoon ground red pepper
1/8	teaspoon cinnamon
1/8	teaspoon ground cloves
1/4	cup fat-free half-and-half
1	tablespoon chopped oregano
1	teaspoon salt
1/4	teaspoon black pepper
2	(15-ounce) cans Great Northern beans, drained and rinsed

Cook the bacon in a Dutch oven over medium heat until crisp. Remove the bacon to paper towels to drain. Crumble the bacon. Drain the Dutch oven, reserving 2 teaspoons of the drippings in the Dutch oven. Add the onion, celery and garlic to the reserved drippings. Cook for 3 minutes or until tender. Add the squash and carrots. Stir in the broth, cumin, red pepper, cinnamon and cloves. Bring to a boil. Reduce the heat and simmer for 5 minutes or until the squash is tender. Stir in the half-and-half, oregano, salt, pepper and beans. Bring to a boil. Remove from the heat. Ladle into soup bowls and sprinkle with the crumbled bacon.

Serves 6

PEAR AND SMOKED GOUDA SALAD

6	to 8 ounces baby spinach, rinsed and chilled	6	tablespoons pecans, chopped
1	cucumber, chilled, peeled and sliced	3/4	cup thinly shaved smoked Gouda cheese
2	Bartlett pears, chilled and thinly sliced		Red wine vinaigrette

Divide the spinach and cucumber evenly among six salad bowls or salad plates. Arrange the pear slices in a pinwheel shape over each portion. Sprinkle 1 tablespoon pecans and 2 tablespoons of the cheese over each portion. Drizzle with vinaigrette and serve with toasted pita points.

Serves 6

TURKEY MELT CASSEROLE

1 1/2	pounds new potatoes	1	bunch Swiss chard, coarsely chopped
2	tablespoons olive oil		
3	garlic cloves, minced	1/2	cup low-fat milk
1	large yellow onion	1/4	cup (1/2 stick) butter
2	cups baby portobello mushrooms, sliced		Salt and pepper to taste
1	pound boneless skinless turkey breast, cut into chunks	2	cups (8 ounces) shredded Cheddar cheese

Place the potatoes in a large saucepan. Add enough water to cover the potatoes by 2 inches. Bring to a boil. Cook until the potatoes are tender. Heat the olive oil a large skillet over medium-high heat. Add the garlic, onion and mushrooms. Sauté for 4 to 5 minutes or until tender. Add the turkey. Cook for 8 minutes or until cooked through, stirring frequently. Add the chard. Cook, covered, for 2 minutes or until the chard is wilted. Remove from the heat and set aside.

Preheat the broiler. Drain the potatoes and return to the saucepan. Add the milk, butter, salt and pepper and mash to the desired consistency. Spread in a thick layer on an ovenproof serving platter. Spoon the turkey mixture over the potatoes. Top with the cheese. Broil for 1 to 2 minutes or until the cheese melts. For a vegetarian dish, add more mushrooms and chard and omit the turkey.

Serves 4

SHRIMP AND GRITS

ROASTED TOMATOES
3	small vine-ripened tomatoes, sliced
1/2	teaspoon kosher salt
1/2	teaspoon pepper
1 1/2	teaspoons olive oil

GRITS
4	cups water
2	teaspoons kosher salt
1	cup quick-cooking grits
2	tablespoons butter
1/4	teaspoon pepper
1/2	cup half-and-half

SHRIMP
3	tablespoons butter
1	onion, chopped
1	cup chopped green bell pepper
1/2	teaspoon kosher salt
1/2	teaspoon pepper
1/4	cup dry sherry
1	tablespoon all-purpose flour
1	cup half-and-half
1/2	teaspoon Old Bay seasoning
1	pound shrimp, peeled and deveined

To prepare the tomatoes, place the tomatoes on a baking sheet. Season with the kosher salt and pepper. Drizzle with the olive oil and toss to coat. Bake in a preheated 400-degree oven for 30 minutes. Remove from the oven and set aside.

To prepare the grits, bring the water and kosher salt to a gentle boil in a medium saucepan. Add the grits gradually. Reduce the heat. Simmer for 5 to 10 minutes or until thickened, stirring frequently. Remove from the heat. Stir in the butter, pepper and half-and-half. Cover and let stand until serving time.

To prepare the shrimp, melt the butter in a large skillet over medium-high heat. Add the onion, bell pepper, kosher salt and pepper. Sauté for 5 minutes. Stir in the sherry, flour, half-and-half and Old Bay seasoning. Cook until thickened, stirring constantly. Add the shrimp. Sauté for 3 minutes or until the shrimp turn pink. Remove from the heat.

To serve, spoon the grits onto serving plates. Top with the roasted tomatoes and shrimp.

Serves 6

FLOTILLA CHILI

1	pound lean ground beef
Olive oil	
1	large onion, chopped
1	green bell pepper, chopped
4	garlic cloves, finely chopped
1	(28-ounce) can tomatoes, chopped
1	(14-ounce) can light red kidney beans
1	(14-ounce) can dark red kidney beans
3/4	cup medium-hot salsa
2	tablespoons chili powder
1	teaspoon ground cumin
1	teaspoon oregano
2	tablespoons molasses
1	(12-ounce) bottle beer, or
	1 (14-ounce) can beef stock

Salt and pepper to taste

Hot pepper sauce to taste

Chili powder to taste

Brown the ground beef in a skillet, stirring until crumbly; drain. Heat olive oil in a large stockpot. Add the onion, bell pepper and garlic. Sauté for 5 minutes. Add the ground beef, tomatoes, beans, salsa, 2 tablespoons chili powder, the cumin, oregano, molasses and beer and mix well. Simmer over low heat for 2 hours. Add the salt, pepper, hot sauce and chili powder to taste and mix well. Ladle into soup bowls. Top with shredded cheese, sour cream, chopped scallions and/or chopped jalapeño chiles.

Serves 6

BROCCOLI CORN BREAD

1	(9-ounce) package corn muffin mix	1	(10-ounce) package frozen chopped broccoli, thawed and drained
4	eggs		
1/2	cup (1 stick) butter, melted	8	ounces cottage cheese

Combine the corn muffin mix, eggs, butter, broccoli and cottage cheese in a bowl and mix well. Pour into a greased 9×13-inch glass baking dish. Bake in a preheated 350-degree oven for 35 to 45 minutes or until golden brown. Cut into squares.

Serves 8 to 10

CORN AND CHEESE FRITTERS

SALSA		1	teaspoon baking powder
1	cup chopped seeded plum tomatoes	3/4	teaspoon ground cumin
			Dash of cayenne pepper
1/3	cup chopped Vidalia onion	1 1/4	cups (5 ounces) shredded Pepper Jack cheese
1	tablespoon chopped cilantro	4	ounces jalapeño chiles, chopped
1	tablespoon fresh lime juice	1	(15-ounce) can whole kernel corn, drained
FRITTERS		2	tablespoons vegetable oil
1	cup all-purpose flour	1 1/2	cups buttermilk
1	cup cornmeal	1/4	cup (1/2 stick) butter
1/2	teaspoon salt		

To prepare the salsa, combine the tomatoes, onion, cilantro and lime juice in a bowl and mix well. Let stand for 15 minutes for the flavors to meld.

To prepare the fritters, combine the flour, cornmeal, salt, baking powder, cumin and cayenne pepper in a mixing bowl. Stir in the cheese, jalapeño chiles and corn. Make a well in the center. Add the oil and buttermilk and stir until combined. Melt enough of the butter to cover the bottom of a skillet. Drop 1/3 cup batter at a time into the hot butter. Cook over medium heat until golden brown on each side. Remove to paper towels to drain. Serve with the salsa and sour cream. Any leftovers can be reheated in the oven.

Serves 8

RUM CAKE

Crushed pecans (optional)
1   (2-layer) package butter recipe yellow cake mix
1   (4-ounce) package vanilla instant pudding mix
4   eggs
3/4   cup rum
1/2   cup vegetable oil
3/4   cup water
1/2   cup (1 stick) margarine
1   cup sugar

Cover the bottom and side of a bundt pan with nonstick cooking spray and sprinkle with pecans. Combine the cake mix, pudding mix, eggs, rum, oil and water in a mixing bowl and beat until smooth. Spoon into the prepared pan. Bake in a preheated 325-degree oven for 1 hour. Bring the margarine and sugar to a boil in a saucepan. Pour over the hot cake in the pan. Let stand until cool. Invert onto a serving plate.

Serves 12

MUD PIE

1/2   cup (1 stick) butter, melted
1   cup (6 ounces) chocolate chips
1/2   cup all-purpose flour
1/2   cup granulated sugar
1/2   cup packed brown sugar
2   eggs, beaten
1   teaspoon vanilla extract
1   cup pecans, chopped
1   unbaked (9-inch) pie shell

Pour the warm melted butter over the chocolate chips in a large bowl and stir until smooth. Mix the flour, granulated sugar, brown sugar, eggs, vanilla and pecans in a bowl. Add to the chocolate mixture and mix well. Spoon into the pie shell. Bake in a preheated 350-degree oven for 30 to 40 minutes or until set.

Serves 8

Holiday Traditions

December is an exciting and magical time in coastal North Carolina. This special month provides opportunities to visit with family and friends, do some holiday shopping, attend seasonal parties, and enjoy an abundance of great food.

To prepare for the holiday festivities, locals head to The Fisherman's Wife in Wrightsville Beach. This delightful retail destination offers all the decorating necessities for adorning your table and home for the holidays. Whimsical tree ornaments, stunning china, and lovely linens abound for both casual and more upscale tastes.

Visitors to the area enjoy special events in December, including:

Old Wilmington by Candlelight — During the first weekend in December, the Historical Society of the Lower Cape Fear holds this self-guided walking tour of some of the beautiful Victorian homes of the Wilmington Historic District.

World's Largest Living Christmas Tree — Located in Wilmington's Hilton Park, the huge oak tree is over 400 years old. The tree is adorned with more than 5,250 lights and was first decorated in 1928. Santa's Shop is nestled under the branches of the magnificent tree.

Enchanted Airlie — A portion of Airlie Gardens is decorated with holiday lights for an opportunity to celebrate the season under the stars. As visitors participate in the self-guided tour, they can enjoy refreshments and live music.

Island of Lights Festival — A month-long festival in Carolina and Kure Beach features an annual Christmas parade with Santa Claus, floats, and bands as well as a tour of homes and a flotilla. Each year a specially designed tree ornament commemorates the holiday season at the beach.

Please join Supper Club

for a

Traditional Holiday Dinner

Saturday, December 3rd

7 o'clock

210 Pelican Drive

regrets

Lib and Joe

Holiday Traditions

Holiday Hopper & Brandy Alexander   140

Oceanic's Famous Crab Dip & Snowman Cheese Ball   141

Beef Tenderloin Steaks with Cranberry Port Sauce and Gorgonzola   142

Perfect Prime Rib & Pineapple Ham   143

Roasted Leg of Lamb & Fennel Lamb Jus   144

Stuffed Onions & Truffle Mashed Potatoes   145

Spinach Casserole & Butternut Squash Risotto   146

Sweet Potato Orange Cups & Holiday Trifle   147

White Wine Cake   148

Coconut Custard Pie & Fisherman's Wife Pecan Pie   149

Chocolate Chip Cream Cheese Ball & Chocolate Rolo Cookies   150

Strawberry-Almond Thumbprint Cookies   151

HOLIDAY HOPPER

2   cups ice cubes
6   ounces green crème de menthe
6   ounces white crème de cacao
6   ounces light cream
Shaved chocolate for garnish

Place enough of the ice cubes in a blender container to fill halfway. Add the crème de menthe, crème de cacao and light cream and process until blended. Add additional ice cubes and process if the consistency is too thin. Pour into martini glasses and garnish with shaved chocolate.

Serves 6

BRANDY ALEXANDER

2   cups ice cubes
6   ounces brandy
6   ounces white crème de menthe
6   ounces light cream
Grated fresh nutmeg for garnish

Place enough of the ice cubes in a blender container to fill halfway. Add the brandy, crème de menthe and light cream and process until blended. Add additional ice cubes and process if the consistency is too thin. Pour into martini glasses and garnish with nutmeg.

Serves 6

OCEANIC'S FAMOUS CRAB DIP

1	tablespoon minced garlic		1	tablespoon fresh lemon juice
2	tablespoons butter		1	tablespoon horseradish
1	tablespoon all-purpose flour		2	dashes of Tabasco sauce
				Salt and pepper to taste
1	cup mayonnaise		1	pound back-fin crab meat, shells removed and meat flaked
8	ounces cream cheese, softened			

Sauté the garlic in the butter in a skillet until tender. Add the flour. Cook for 5 minutes, stirring constantly. Remove from the heat. Stir in the mayonnaise, cream cheese, lemon juice, horseradish, Tabasco sauce, salt and pepper. Fold in the crab meat. Spoon into a baking dish. Bake in a preheated 375-degree oven for 15 minutes or until bubbly and golden brown.

Note: Renowned for their panoramic ocean views and seafood specialties and steaks, the Oceanic Restaurant is a local favorite and a must-see for visitors.

Serves 4

SNOWMAN CHEESE BALL

24	ounces cream cheese, softened		1/4	teaspoon dry mustard
4	cups (16 ounces) shredded Cheddar cheese		2	dashes of hot pepper sauce
1	cup (4 ounces) shredded mozzarella cheese		1/4	cup finely chopped fresh parsley
2	tablespoons pesto		1/16	teaspoon garlic powder
1	tablespoon dried grated onion		1/3	cup blanched almonds
			2	pretzel sticks

Combine the cream cheese, Cheddar cheese, mozzarella cheese, pesto, onion, dry mustard, hot sauce, parsley and garlic powder in a bowl and mix well. Divide into two portions, with one portion being slightly smaller than the other. Chill for 4 hours. Shape each portion into a ball and coat in the almonds. Arrange the balls on a serving plate with the smallest ball on top of the largest one to resemble a snowman and lightly press together. Insert pretzel sticks for the arms. Decorate as desired forming eyes, nose, mouth and buttons. Serve with assorted crackers.

Serves 10 to 12

BEEF TENDERLOIN STEAKS WITH CRANBERRY PORT SAUCE AND GORGONZOLA

2	tablespoons butter
2	large garlic cloves, sliced
1	large shallot, sliced
1	cup beef broth
1	cup ruby port
1/4	cup dried cranberries
4	(5- to 6-ounce) beef tenderloin steaks, 1 inch thick

Salt and pepper to taste

2	tablespoons butter
1/2	teaspoon minced fresh rosemary
1/4	cup beef broth
1/2	cup crumbled gorgonzola cheese

Melt 2 tablespoons butter in a saucepan over medium-high heat. Add the garlic, shallot, 1 cup broth, the wine and dried cranberries. Boil for 8 minutes or until reduced to 1/2 cup. Remove from the heat. Sprinkle the steaks with salt and pepper. Melt 2 tablespoons butter in a large skillet over medium-high heat. Add the steaks. Cook for 5 minutes on each side for medium-rare or to the desired degree of doneness. Remove the steaks to a platter and cover loosely with foil. Add the rosemary to the drippings in the skillet. Stir in the cranberry port sauce and 1/4 cup broth. Boil for 1 minute, stirring to deglaze the skillet. Sprinkle with salt and pepper. Spoon over the steaks. Sprinkle with the cheese.

Serves 4

Perfect Prime Rib

1   tablespoon olive oil
1 1/2 teaspoons kosher salt
1   teaspoon pepper
1   (6-pound) prime rib roast

Combine the olive oil, kosher salt and pepper in a small bowl and stir to mix well. Rub evenly over the roast. Place the roast on a wire rack in a foil-lined roasting pan. Bake in a preheated 450-degree oven for 45 minutes. Reduce the oven temperature to 350 degrees. Bake for 45 minutes or to 145 degrees on a meat thermometer. Let stand, loosely covered with foil, for 20 minutes before serving.

Note: Serve with Horseradish Sauce, which is made by whisking 1 part horseradish and 2 parts sour cream together.

Serves 12 to 15

Pineapple Ham

3/4 cup undrained crushed pineapple
1/2 cup Dijon mustard
1/2 cup honey
1   tablespoon all-purpose flour
1   (8- to 10-pound) semi-boneless ham

Mix the pineapple, Dijon mustard and honey in a bowl. Sprinkle the flour in a large browning bag. Place the ham in the prepared bag. Pour the pineapple mixture over the ham and seal the bag. Rub the bag to spread the pineapple mixture over the ham to coat. Place in a 9×13-inch glass baking dish. Cut three or four slits in the top of the bag to allow the steam to escape. Bake in a preheated 225-degree oven for 8 to 10 hours. Remove from the oven to cool. Cut into slices.

Note: Some gourmet food stores sell premade pineapple mustard dip. If you prefer to use premade sauce, you will need 1/2 cup for this recipe. If the honey is difficult to mix, microwave for 10 seconds and mix well. Do not use a metal pan in this recipe because the results will not be the same.

Serves 16 to 20

ROASTED LEG OF LAMB

1   (2-pound) top round leg of lamb

Salt and pepper to taste

1   cup Fennel Lamb Jus (below)

1/4   cup basil oil for garnish

Tapenade crostini for garnish (about 4 per person)

Sprinkle the lamb with salt and pepper. Place on a rack in a roasting pan. Roast in a preheated 350-degree oven for 25 to 30 minutes or to 145 degrees on a meat thermometer for medium-rare. Remove from the oven and let stand for 10 minutes. Cut into thin slices and place on serving plates. Drizzle the Fennel Lamb Jus over the lamb. Garnish with the basil oil and tapenade crostini.

Serves 4

FENNEL LAMB JUS

Lamb bones

Mirepoix vegetables (50% onions, 25% carrots, 25% celery)

Tomato paste

Water

Bay leaves

Fresh rosemary

Toasted fennel seeds

Black peppercorns

Parsley

Roast the lamb bones in a roasting pan in a preheated 350-degree oven until well caramelized. Remove the lamb bones to a stockpot and set aside. Add the mirepoix to the drippings in the roasting pan and sauté until brown. Stir in tomato paste. Add water, stirring to deglaze the pan. Spoon the mixture into the stockpot. Add bay leaves, rosemary, fennel seeds, peppercorns and parsley. Bring to a boil. Reduce the heat and simmer for 2 to 3 hours. Strain through a chinoise. Adjust the seasonings and thickness of the jus.

Note: As an alternative to roasting lamb bones, you may purchase lamb stock, which is available in gourmet grocery stores. Brown the vegetables and proceed as directed above.

Makes a variable amount

STUFFED ONIONS

8   white onions

Salt to taste

10   slices dry white bread, crumbled

1   pint (2 cups) heavy whipping cream

Cooking sherry to taste

1   pound mild bulk sausage

2   teaspoons thyme

1/4   cup (1/2 stick) butter

1   cup beef bouillon

Trim off the ends of the onions. Blanch the onions in salted water in a
large saucepan until tender; drain. Core the onions, leaving about three layers
intact. Chop some of the onion centers and set aside. Reserve the remaining onion
for another use. Soak the bread in the cream and sherry in a large bowl.

Brown the sausage, chopped onion and thyme in a skillet, stirring until
crumbly; drain. Stir in the bread mixture. Simmer for 2 to 3 minutes over
medium heat. Stuff into the cored onions and place in a shallow glass baking
dish. Top each stuffed onion with 1/2 tablespoon of the butter. Pour the bouillon
around the onions. Bake in a preheated 400-degree oven for 45 minutes, basting
occasionally with the bouillon.

Serves 8

TRUFFLE MASHED POTATOES

2   pounds Yukon Gold potatoes, peeled and chopped

1   cup (2 sticks) butter

2   cups half-and-half

1/4   cup white truffle oil

Salt and pepper to taste

Cook the potatoes in boiling water in a saucepan until tender; drain.
Mash the potatoes in a mixing bowl. Melt the butter in a saucepan. Add the
half-and-half. Add to the warm potatoes. Add the truffle oil, salt and pepper and
mix well.

Serves 6

SPINACH CASSEROLE

3	(10-ounce) packages frozen chopped spinach
3	slices bacon, cooked and crumbled
6	ounces sliced mushrooms
1/2	teaspoon salt
1/4	teaspoon pepper
1	cup sour cream
1/2	cup (2 ounces) shredded sharp Cheddar cheese

Cook the spinach using the package directions; drain. Add the bacon, mushrooms, salt and pepper. Spread in a buttered 7×11-inch baking dish. Cover with the sour cream. Sprinkle with the cheese. Bake in a preheated 350-degree oven for 20 minutes.

Serves 8 to 10

BUTTERNUT SQUASH RISOTTO

1	pound butternut squash, peeled
8	cups vegetable broth or chicken broth
1/4	cup (1/2 stick) butter, softened
11/2	cups finely chopped yellow or Vidalia onions
2	cups short-grain arborio rice
1/2	cup white wine
3/4	cup (3 ounces) grated Parmesan cheese
1/4	cup whipping cream

Salt and pepper to taste

Cut the squash into 1/2-inch pieces. Bring the broth to a boil in a large saucepan. Cover and reduce the heat to low. Melt the butter in a large Dutch oven over medium heat. Add the onions and sauté until tender. Add the squash and cook for 3 minutes. Add the rice and cook for 2 minutes. Stir in the wine. Cook for 1 minute. Bring to a boil; reduce the heat to low. Add 1/2 cup of the hot broth. Cook until the broth is absorbed, stirring constantly. Repeat with the remaining broth 1/2 cup at a time until all the broth has been added and the rice is creamy. Stir in the cheese, cream, salt and pepper. Serve immediately.

Serves 6 to 8

SWEET POTATO ORANGE CUPS

6	to 8 oranges
3	large cans sweet potatoes
1/2	cup (1 stick) butter, melted
1/4	cup packed brown sugar
1	cup whipping cream

Marshmallows

Cut the top from each orange and hollow out with a spoon, reserving 1/2 to 1 cup of the orange sections. Beat the sweet potatoes, butter and brown sugar in a mixing bowl until light and fluffy. Beat in the cream and reserved orange sections gradually. Spoon into the orange cups, leaving room at the top for expansion. Place in a baking dish. Bake in a preheated 350-degree oven for 10 to 15 minutes. Top with marshmallows. Broil for 1 minute or until brown.

Serves 6 to 8

HOLIDAY TRIFLE

1	(4-ounce) package cook-and-serve vanilla pudding mix
1	(4-ounce) package cook-and-serve coconut pudding mix
2	cups fresh or frozen strawberries, sliced
1 1/2	cups fresh or frozen blueberries
3/4	cup peach schnapps
1	angel food cake, torn into large pieces
3	cups whipped topping

Fresh strawberries and blueberries for garnish

Combine and prepare the pudding mixes using the package directions. Soak the strawberries and blueberries in the liqueur in a large bowl. Layer the cake, fruit mixture, pudding and whipped topping one-half at a time in a large glass trifle bowl or serving bowl. Garnish with fresh strawberries and blueberries.

Serves 8

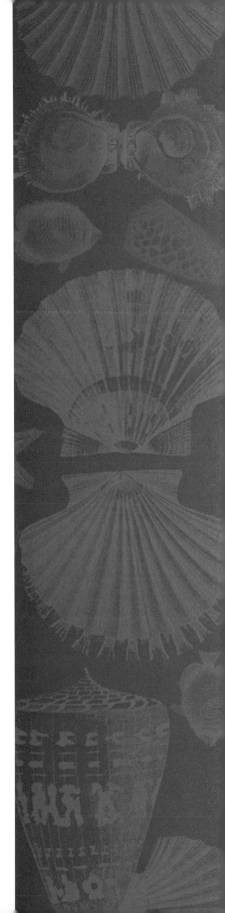

WHITE WINE CAKE

CAKE

1/4	cup pecans, chopped
1	(2-layer) package yellow cake mix
1	(3-ounce) package vanilla instant pudding mix
1/2	cup water
1/2	cup white wine
3/4	cup vegetable oil
4	eggs
1/4	cup packed brown sugar
1/4	cup granulated sugar
2	teaspoons cinnamon
1/2	cup pecans, chopped

WHITE WINE GLAZE

1/2	cup (1 stick) butter or margarine
3/4	cup sugar
1/4	cup water
1/4	cup pecans, chopped
1/4	cup white wine

To prepare the cake, sprinkle 1/4 cup pecans in a greased and floured bundt pan or tube pan. Combine the cake mix, pudding mix, water, wine, oil, eggs, brown sugar, granulated sugar and cinnamon in a mixing bowl and beat at low speed until smooth. Stir in 1/2 cup pecans. Spoon into the prepared pan. Bake in a preheated 350-degree oven for 1 hour.

To prepare the glaze, bring the butter, sugar, water and pecans to a boil in a saucepan. Boil for 2 to 3 minutes. Stir in the wine and remove from the heat.

To assemble, remove the cake from the oven. Pour one-half of the glaze over the hot cake in the pan. Let stand for 10 minutes. Invert onto a cake plate. Pour the remaining glaze over the top. Serve warm.

Serves 12

Coconut Custard Pie

1/4   cup (1/2 stick) unsalted butter, softened

1   cup sugar

3   egg whites

1/2   cup evaporated milk

1   teaspoon vanilla extract

Pinch of salt

1   (7-ounce) package shredded coconut

1   unbaked (9-inch) pie shell

Beat the butter, sugar, egg whites, evaporated milk, vanilla and salt in a mixing bowl until smooth. Stir in the coconut. Pour into the pie shell. Bake in a preheated 350-degree oven for 20 minutes. Reduce the oven temperature to 325 degrees. Bake for 20 minutes longer.

Serves 6 to 8

Fisherman's Wife Pecan Pie

3   eggs

1   cup dark corn syrup

1/2   cup sugar

2   tablespoons butter, melted

2   teaspoons vanilla extract

1/4   teaspoon salt

1   cup pecans, chopped

1   unbaked (9-inch) pie shell

Combine the eggs, corn syrup, sugar, butter, vanilla and salt in a bowl and mix well. Stir in the pecans. Pour into the pie shell. Bake in a preheated 350-degree oven for 50 minutes or until set.

Serves 6 to 8

CHOCOLATE CHIP CREAM CHEESE BALL

8	ounces cream cheese, softened	3/4	cup miniature semisweet chocolate chips
1/2	cup (1 stick) butter, softened	3/4	cup pecans, chopped
1/4	teaspoon vanilla extract		Maraschino cherries, cut into slivers
3/4	cup confectioners' sugar		
2	tablespoons light brown sugar		

Beat the cream cheese, butter and vanilla in a mixing bowl until fluffy. Add the confectioners' sugar and brown sugar gradually, beating constantly. Stir in the chocolate chips. Chill, covered, for 2 hours. Shape into a ball. Chill, covered, for 1 hour longer. Roll in the pecans to coat and place on a serving plate. Arrange maraschino cherry slivers on the outside of the ball. Serve with graham crackers.

Serves 8 to 10

CHOCOLATE ROLO COOKIES

1	(2-layer) package German chocolate cake mix	3	tablespoons vegetable oil
1/4	cup water	1	(12-ounce) package Rolo candies
1	egg		

Combine the cake mix, water, egg and oil in a bowl and mix well. Spray your fingers with nonstick cooking spray and shape the mixture by teaspoonfuls into balls. Place one candy in each ball and reshape into a ball. Place on an ungreased cookie sheet. Bake in a preheated 350-degree oven for 10 minutes. Cool on a wire rack.

Makes 2 dozen

STRAWBERRY-ALMOND THUMBPRINT COOKIES

COOKIES

1   cup (2 sticks) butter, softened

2/3   cup sugar

1/2   teaspoon almond extract

2   cups all-purpose flour

Strawberry preserves

ALMOND GLAZE

1 1/2 cups confectioners' sugar

2   teaspoons almond extract

4   or 5 teaspoons water

To prepare the cookies, microwave the butter in a microwave-safe bowl on High until melted. Add the sugar, almond extract and flour and mix well. Shape into 1- to 2-inch balls and place on a cookie sheet. Press your thumb in the center of each ball to form an indentation. Fill with strawberry preserves. Bake in a preheated 350-degree oven for 14 to 18 minutes or until light brown. Cool on a wire rack.

To prepare the glaze, combine the confectioners' sugar, almond extract and water in a bowl and mix until smooth. Drizzle over the cooled cookies.

Makes 3 dozen

SPONSORS

The Junior League of Wilmington, NC, Inc., gratefully acknowledges the financial and in-kind support of the following businesses and individual friends, as their assistance exemplifies their concern and commitment to the children and families of our community. The beauty of this book was enhanced by their offerings of props to adorn the table, sites for location shots, and a lovely beach home setting in which to sample the tasty recipes presented in this rich volume of culinary delights.

Airlie Gardens

Chef James Bain, Dockside Restaurant

Bangz Hair Salon

Carolina Yacht Club

Joshua Curry, Photographer

Herend Fine Dinnerware

Oceanic Restaurant

The Reel Café

Jane Metts Rippy

Celia Rivenbark

Connie Smith

Uptown Market

Estelle Baker, Dorothy Bridger, Laura Smith, The Fisherman's Wife

CONTRIBUTORS

The Junior League of Wilmington, NC, Inc., is very grateful for the active members who offered their time and talents so that the League's cookbook tradition could continue through this culinary text. The committed and loving preparation of this book involved many League members over the course of two years, and their work is much appreciated.

Devon Baldwin
Kathleen Beaman
Kelly Bowers
Rebecca Bowman
Amanda Bullock
Elena Cazeault
Kelley Evans
Katie Faulkner
Jill Gunter
Anna Jarrell
Christy Kramer
Jennifer MacKethan
Emily McNamara
Kristie Pate
Taylor Simms

A special thank-you goes to the contributions of Juliet Lee, Karen Kirk, Adrienne McTigue, and Lisa Menius, whose extra efforts ensured the completion of this book for all to savor—both for the brilliant photography and the edible delights. These women embody the Spirit of the League!

CONTRIBUTORS

The delectable recipes included in *Seaboard to Sideboard Entertains* were offered by businesses and individuals who share a passion for entertaining. Every recipe was tested by our members to ensure accuracy and clarity. The Junior League of Wilmington expresses gratitude to everyone who contributed their efforts so generously. We hope that we have listed everyone who contributed to the success of this book; we genuinely apologize if we omitted anyone's name unintentionally.

Airlie Gardens

Jimmy Albertson
Betsy Albright
Joy Alford-Brand
Annie Anthony
James Bain
Estelle Baker
Devon Baldwin
Terrie Boggs
Kelly Bowers
Logan Bradshaw
Shan Brown
Jennifer Bullock
Elena Cazeault
Angela Cline
Michelle Daniel
Grace Davis
May Deeb
Susan M. DeGroote
Ellen DiLorenzo
Amy Evans
Kelley Evans
Jennifer Fletcher

Oceanic Restaurant

Aimee Gianoukos
Sarah Gregory
Jill Davis Gunter
Jamie Hamm
Curtis Hensyl
Patty Jensen
Caite Kempf
Karen Kirk
Christy Kramer
Juliet Lee
Laura Lee
Nancy Lee
Whitney Leonard
Mary Lisa Lindstrom
Jennifer MacKethan
Christian Swiers Marini
Ragda McAfee
Dawn McKernan
Meredith McSwain
Adrienne McTigue
Lisa Menius
Tracee Meyer
Sue Murphy

Dockside Restaurant

Dana O'Donovan
Kristie Pate
Jennifer Grau Patterson
Crystal Peebles
Alyce Phillips
Maggie Cromer Prater
Elizabeth Redenbaugh
Jessica Reed
Jessica Riffle
Jane Metts Rippy
Helen Rittersporn
Celia Rivenbark
Katie Roy
Virginia Rynk
Sarah Shay
Melissa Smith
Rania Smith
Katie Lee Tartt
Lucy West
Cassie Williamson
Shannon Wilson
Amy Wright

INDEX

Accompaniments. *See also*
    Sauces; Salsas
    Mint Whipped Cream, 43
    Pepper Jelly Sauce, 95
    Roasted Tomatoes, 132

Appetizers. *See also* Dips; Salsas;
    Spreads
    Bacon Almond Crostini, 26
    Blue Cheese Bread, 28
    Cheddar en Croûte, 14
    Cheese Crispies, 72
    Hot Cheese Squares, 104
    Pizza Bread, 110
    Sausage Bites, 105
    Seaside Gougères, 49
    Vodka-Infused Tomatoes, 50

Artichokes
    Baked Shrimp and
        Artichoke Dip, 61
    Crab and Artichoke Dip, 15

Asparagus
    Cream of Oyster Stew, 17
    Oven-Roasted Asparagus, 32

Avocado
    Avocado and Corn Salsa, 92
    Old Baldy Pasta Salad, 85

Bacon
    Bacon Almond Crostini, 26
    Bacon Cheddar Deviled Eggs, 83
    Breakfast Squares, 39
    Broccoli Salad, 86
    Hot Swiss Bacon Dip, 15
    Warm Potato Salad with Arugula
        and Bacon, 93

Banana
    Banana Pudding, 122
    Sour Cream Banana Bread, 41

Beans
    Autumn Squash Soup, 130
    Black Bean Chili, 109
    Black Bean Dip, 73
    Brunswick Stew, 19
    Corn Relish Salad, 120
    Flotilla Chili, 133
    Hummus, 27

    Seahawk Salsa, 106
    Summer Bean Dip, 82
    Tangy Green Beans with
        Pimento, 98
    Three-Bean Baked Beans, 121
    White Chicken Chili, 30

Beef
    Beef or Chicken Kabobs, 110
    Beef Tenderloin Steaks with
        Cranberry Port Sauce and
        Gorgonzola, 142
    Black Bean Chili, 109
    Flotilla Chili, 133
    Mini Meat Loaves, 31
    Perfect Prime Rib, 143
    Sweet-and-Savory Slider
        Burgers, 84
    Three-Bean Baked Beans, 121

Beverages
    Azalea Punch, 48
    Basil-Infused Watermelon
        Lemonade, 82
    Brandy Alexander, 140
    Flo-tini, 128
    Frozen Margarita Punch, 60
    Holiday Hopper, 140
    Honeydew and Lemon Grass
        Soda Water, 48
    Jubilee Julep, 60
    Mint Iced Tea, 72
    Mulled Red Wine, 14
    Perfect Punch, 38
    Southern Sweet Tea, 116
    Tarheel Tea, 104

Blueberry
    Blueberry Cobbler, 87
    Holiday Trifle, 147

Breads
    Blue Cheese Bread, 28
    Broccoli Corn Bread, 134
    Pizza Bread, 110
    Pumpkin Biscuits with
        Maple Ham, 122
    Sour Cream Banana Bread, 41

Broccoli
    Broccoli Corn Bread, 134
    Broccoli Salad, 86

    Creamy Chicken and
        Broccoli Bake, 30
    Old Baldy Pasta Salad, 86

Cabbage
    Barbecue Slaw, 120
    Picnic Slaw, 75

Cakes
    Chocolate Chip Cake, 55
    Favorite Chocolate Cake, 123
    Rum Cake, 135
    Southern Pound Cake, 42
    White Wine Cake, 148

Carrots
    Farmers' Market Dip, 38
    Pasta Salad, 76

Cheddar Cheese
    Bacon Cheddar Deviled Eggs, 83
    Best-Ever Cheese Ring, 116
    Cheddar en Croûte, 14
    Cheese Crispies, 72
    Hot Cheese Squares, 104
    Jalapeño Pimento Cheese, 74
    Pimento Cheese Sandwiches, 53
    Rosemary Pimento Cheese
        Sandwiches, 53
    White Cheddar Pimento Cheese
        Sandwiches, 54

Cheese. *See also* Cheddar Cheese
    Blue Cheese Bread, 28
    Blue Crab and Brie Fondue, 39
    Corn and Cheese Fritters, 134
    Cream Cheese with Apricot
        Preserves, 51
    Hot Swiss Bacon Dip, 15
    Pear and Smoked Gouda
        Salad, 131
    Pineapple Cheese Ball, 62
    Snowman Cheese Ball, 141

Chicken
    Beef or Chicken Kabobs, 110
    Brunswick Stew, 19
    Buffalo Chicken Dip, 106
    Buttermilk Fried Chicken, 85
    Chicken and Arugula
        Roll-Ups, 40
    Chicken Burgers, 84

Chicken Chimichanga Dip, 129
Creamy Chicken and
    Broccoli Bake, 30
Curried Chicken Salad, 73
White Chicken Chili, 30

Chili
Black Bean Chili, 109
Flotilla Chili, 133
White Chicken Chili, 30

Chocolate
Beach Brownies, 77
Cheesecake Brownies, 21
Cherry Chocolate Oatmeal
    Cookies, 77
Chocolate Chip Cake, 55
Chocolate Chip Cream
    Cheese Ball, 150
Chocolate Pecan Squares, 33
Chocolate Rolo Cookies, 151
Crazy-Good Peanut Butter
    Pie, 111
Favorite Chocolate Cake, 123
Game Day Cookies, 111
Mud Pie, 135
Oatmeal Caramel Cranberry
    Cookies, 21

Cookies
Cherry Chocolate Oatmeal
    Cookies, 77
Chocolate Rolo Cookies, 151
Game Day Cookies, 111
Lemon Butter Cookies, 43
Oatmeal Caramel Cranberry
    Cookies, 21
Strawberry-Almond Thumbprint
    Cookies, 150

Cookies, Bar
Beach Brownies, 77
Cheesecake Brownies, 21
Chess Squares, 55
Chocolate Pecan Squares, 33
Lemon Squares, 42

Corn
Avocado and Corn Salsa, 92
Black Bean Dip, 73
Brunswick Stew, 19
Corn and Cheese Fritters, 134

Corn Relish Salad, 120
Country Ham and Corn Sauté, 95
Grilled Corn and Crab Salad, 85
Seahawk Salsa, 106
Tropical Edamame Salad, 119

Crab Meat
Blue Crab and Brie Fondue, 39
Cape Fear Crab Cakes, 64
Carolina Crab Dip, 50
Crab and Artichoke Dip, 15
Crab Bake, 128
Grilled Corn and Crab Salad, 85
Oceanic's Famous Crab Dip, 141
Seaside Gougères, 49

Cranberry
Azalea Punch, 48
Beef Tenderloin Steaks with
    Cranberry Port Sauce and
    Gorgonzola, 142
Broccoli Salad, 86
Oatmeal Caramel Cranberry
    Cookies, 21

Cucumber
Cucumber-Watercress Tea
    Sandwiches, 52
Gazpacho, 94
Pasta Salad, 76
Refrigerator Pickles, 76

Desserts. *See also* Cakes; Cookies;
    Icings/Glazes; Pies
Banana Pudding, 122
Blueberry Cobbler, 87
Chocolate Chip Cream
    Cheese Ball, 150
Devonshire Grapes, 54
Grilled Fruit Kabobs, 66
Holiday Trifle, 147
Peach Crisp, 87
Roasted Strawberries with
    Lemon Butter Cookies and
    Mint Whipped Cream, 43

Dips
Baked Shrimp and Artichoke
    Dip, 61
Black Bean Dip, 73
Blue Crab and Brie Fondue, 39
Buffalo Chicken Dip, 106

Carolina Crab Dip, 50
Chicken Chimichanga Dip, 129
Crab and Artichoke Dip, 15
Farmers' Market Dip, 38
Hot Swiss Bacon Dip, 15
Italian Layer Dip, 105
Oceanic's Famous Crab Dip, 141
Seven-Layer Shrimp Dip, 61
Spinach Tomato Dip, 51
Summer Bean Dip, 82

Edamame
Peanut and Edamame Stew, 29
Tropical Edamame Salad, 119

Egg Dishes
Bacon Cheddar Deviled
    Eggs, 83
Breakfast Squares, 39
Chiles Rellenos Quiche, 40
Spicy Deviled Eggs, 83

Eggplant
Eggplant Caviar, 27
Roasted Vegetable Salad, 63

Fish
Pan-Roasted Grouper with
    Country Ham and Corn Sauté
    and Pepper Jelly Sauce, 95
Seafood Pot, 18

Fruit. *See also* Individual kinds
Cherry Chocolate Oatmeal
    Cookies, 77
Cream Cheese with Apricot
    Preserves, 51
Devonshire Grapes, 54
Grilled Fruit Kabobs, 66
Peach Crisp, 87
Pear and Smoked Gouda
    Salad, 131
Pumpkin Biscuits with
    Maple Ham, 122
Tropical Edamame Salad, 119

Ham
Country Ham and Corn Sauté, 95
Pasta Salad, 76
Pineapple Ham, 143
Pumpkin Biscuits with
    Maple Ham, 122

Roasted Red Pepper and
    Prosciutto Sandwiches, 75
Stuffed Potatoes, 108

Icings/Glazes
Almond Glaze, 150
Chocolate Icing, 123
White Wine Glaze, 148

Lamb
Fennel Lamb Jus, 144
Roasted Leg of Lamb, 144

Lemon/Lime
Basil-Infused Watermelon
    Lemonade, 82
Easy Key Lime Pie, 67
Grilled Corn and Crab
    Salad, 85
Lemonade Pie, 98
Lemon Butter Cookies, 43
Lemon Squares, 42

Melon
Basil-Infused Watermelon
    Lemonade, 82
Honeydew and Lemon Grass
    Soda Water, 48
Tomato and Watermelon
    Salad, 93

Nuts
Bacon Almond Crostini, 26
Chocolate Pecan Squares, 33
Fisherman's Wife Pecan Pie, 149
Plantation Pie, 99
Riverwalk Salad, 62
Strawberry-Almond Thumbprint
    Cookies, 150
Sweet-and-Spicy Walnuts, 129

Olives
Creamy Olive Spread, 26
Old Baldy Pasta Salad, 86
Roasted Red Pepper and
    Prosciutto Sandwiches, 75

Orange
Ambrosia Salad, 41
Summer Salad with Raspberry
    Vinaigrette, 92
Sweet Potato Orange Cups, 147

Oysters
Cream of Oyster Stew, 17
Low Country EZ Oyster Stew, 16
Oyster Stuffing, 20
Quick-and-Easy Fried Oysters, 20
Wrightsville Beach Oyster Stew, 17

Pasta
Old Baldy Pasta Salad, 86
Pasta Salad, 76
Rigatoni with Sausage and
    Baby Arugula, 94
Spinach Lasagna with
    White Sauce, 31

Peanut Butter
Crazy-Good Peanut Butter
    Pie, 111
Peanut and Edamame Stew, 29
Peanut Butter Pie, 33

Peas
Brunswick Stew, 19
Curried Chicken Salad, 73

Peppers
Avocado and Corn Salsa, 92
Farmers' Market Dip, 38
Gazpacho, 94
Old Baldy Pasta Salad, 86
Pasta Salad, 76
Roasted Red Pepper and
    Prosciutto Sandwiches, 75
Stuffed Potatoes, 108

Pies
Beach Cottage Pie, 66
Coconut Custard Pie, 149
Crazy-Good Peanut Butter
    Pie, 111
Easy Key Lime Pie, 67
Fisherman's Wife Pecan Pie, 149
Lemonade Pie, 98
Mud Pie, 135
Peanut Butter Pie, 33
Plantation Pie, 99
Strawberry Pie, 99
Tomato Pie, 97

Pineapple
Ambrosia Salad, 41
Perfect Punch, 38

Pineapple Cheese Ball, 62
Pineapple Ham, 143
Plantation Pie, 99

Pork. *See also* Bacon; Ham; Sausage
Braised Pork Tenderloin, 65
Brunswick Stew, 19
Fallin'-Off-the-Bone Ribs, 119
Jamaican Jerk Pork Tenderloin, 96
Loaded Barbecue Potato
    Casserole, 118
Traditional Pulled Pork, 117

Potatoes
Brunswick Stew, 19
Grilled Corn and Crab Salad, 85
Loaded Barbecue Potato
    Casserole, 118
Red-Skinned Potatoes with
    Herbs, 32
Stuffed Potatoes, 108
Truffle Mashed Potatoes, 145
Warm Potato Salad with Arugula
    and Bacon, 93

Salads
Ambrosia Salad, 41
Barbecue Slaw, 120
Broccoli Salad, 86
Corn Relish Salad, 120
Curried Chicken Salad, 73
Devonshire Grapes, 54
Grilled Corn and Crab Salad, 85
Old Baldy Pasta Salad, 86
Pasta Salad, 76
Pear and Smoked Gouda
    Salad, 131
Picnic Slaw, 75
Riverwalk Salad, 62
Roasted Vegetable Salad, 63
Spinach Salad, 28
Summer Salad with Raspberry
    Vinaigrette, 92
Tomato and Watermelon Salad, 93
Tropical Edamame Salad, 119
Warm Potato Salad with Arugula
    and Bacon, 93

Salsas
Avocado and Corn Salsa, 92
Salsa, 134
Seahawk Salsa, 106

Sandwiches
Cucumber-Watercress Tea
Sandwiches, 52
Pimento Cheese
Sandwiches, 53
Roasted Red Pepper and
Prosciutto Sandwiches, 75
Rosemary Pimento Cheese
Sandwiches, 53
Sweet-and-Savory Slider
Burgers, 84
White Cheddar Pimento Cheese
Sandwiches, 54

Sauces
Eastern Carolina Barbecue
Sauce, 117
Fennel Lamb Jus, 144
Oyster Sauce, 16
Rémoulade Sauce, 64
Simple Cocktail Sauce, 107

Sausage
Oyster Stuffing, 20
Rigatoni with Sausage and
Baby Arugula, 94
Sausage Bites, 105
Stuffed Onions, 145

Seafood. *See also* Crab Meat; Fish;
Oysters; Shrimp
Seafood Pot, 18

Shrimp
Baked Shrimp and Artichoke
Dip, 61
Seafood Pot, 18
Seven-Layer Shrimp Dip, 61
Shrimp and Grits, 132
Spiced Steamed Shrimp, 107

Side Dishes
Butternut Squash Risotto, 146
Grits, 132
Oyster Stuffing, 20

Soups. *See also* Chili; Stews
Autumn Squash Soup, 130
Gazpacho, 94
Seafood Pot, 18

Spinach
Chicken Burgers, 84
Peanut and Edamame Stew, 29
Pear and Smoked Gouda
Salad, 131
Spinach Casserole, 146
Spinach Lasagna with
White Sauce, 31
Spinach Salad, 28
Spinach Tomato Dip, 51

Spreads
Best-Ever Cheese Ring, 116
Chocolate Chip Cream
Cheese Ball, 150
Crab Bake, 128
Cream Cheese with Apricot
Preserves, 51
Creamy Olive Spread, 26
Eggplant Caviar, 27
Hummus, 27
Jalapeño Pimento Cheese, 74
Pimento Cheese
Sandwiches, 53
Pineapple Cheese Ball, 62
Rosemary Pimento Cheese
Sandwiches, 53
Snowman Cheese Ball, 141
White Cheddar Pimento Cheese
Sandwiches, 54

Squash
Autumn Squash Soup, 130
Butternut Squash Risotto, 146
Roasted Vegetable Salad, 63
Summer Squash Casserole, 97

Stews
Brunswick Stew, 19
Cream of Oyster Stew, 17

Low Country EZ Oyster
Stew, 16
Peanut and Edamame Stew, 29
Wrightsville Beach Oyster
Stew, 17

Strawberry
Holiday Trifle, 147
Roasted Strawberries with
Lemon Butter Cookies and
Mint Whipped Cream, 43
Strawberry-Almond Thumbprint
Cookies, 150
Strawberry Pie, 99
Summer Salad with Raspberry
Vinaigrette, 92

Sweet Potatoes
Peanut and Edamame Stew, 29
Sweet Potato Orange Cups, 147

Tomatoes
Avocado and Corn Salsa, 92
Black Bean Chili, 109
Brunswick Stew, 19
Eggplant Caviar, 27
Flotilla Chili, 133
Gazpacho, 94
Grilled Corn and Crab Salad, 85
Roasted Tomatoes, 132
Salsa, 134
Seafood Pot, 18
Seahawk Salsa, 106
Spinach Tomato Dip, 51
Tomato and Watermelon
Salad, 93
Tomato Pie, 97
Vodka-Infused Tomatoes, 50

Turkey
Turkey Melt Casserole, 131

Vegetables. *See also* Individual kinds
Fresh Collard Greens, 121
Stuffed Onions, 145

SEABOARD TO SIDEBOARD ENTERTAINS

Thank you for your interest in
the Junior League of Wilmington's cookbook series.

Orders for this and other books may be placed by visiting
our Web site at www.jlwnc.org. There you will also find
information about SEABOARD TO SIDEBOARD, the prequel to
SEABOARD TO SIDEBOARD ENTERTAINS.

Or, please call us at 910-799-7405.